Capablanca:
A Primer of Checkmate

Frisco Del Rosario

MONGOOSE
Press

BOSTON

Publisher: Mongoose Press
1005 Boylston Street, Suite 324
Newton Highlands, MA 02461
info@mongoosepress.com
www.MongoosePress.com
ISBN: 978-1-9362770-2-5
Library of Congress Control Number: 2010927465
Distributed to the trade by National Book Network
custserv@nbnbooks.com, 800-462-6420
For all other sales inquiries please contact the Publisher.

Layout: Semko Semkov
Editor: Jorge Amador
Cover Design: Creative Center – Bulgaria
First English edition
0 9 8 7 6 5 4 3 2 1
Printed in China

To my father, Frisco Rolando Del Rosario,
a military man who showed his kid how the pieces move;
and to Richard Shorman, a chess teacher who suggested
that the pieces should cooperate.

Acknowledgements

Thanks to:

My mother, Carol Ann Farrell, for putting the first pen in my hand.

The Kolty Chess Club, for being good opponents, good friends, good audience. Special thanks to Roland Arajs, Chris Black, Matt Benson, Félix Hernández-Campos for their critical reading.

The staff and patrons of Philz Coffee in Palo Alto, California, for extraordinary coffee, energetic atmosphere, music live and recorded. Hi, Brianna!

Software developer Rolf Exner, for the *ExaChess* software.

Peter Biyiasas, two-time Canadian champion, for listening kindly to my talks at the chess club, while inspiring more thorough preparation.

John Grefe, the 1973 U.S. Champion, and Julian Hodgson, a four-time U.K. champion, for encouraging *me* to explain Capablanca to *them*.

Jorge Amador, my editor at Mongoose Press, for sharpening the text and imagining an agreeable title, playing on Capablanca's *A Primer of Chess*.

BayAreaChess and Weibel Chess students and staff.

ChessDryad, for library access; and

My oldest chess friends, the Whistlin' Pig Chess Club.

This book was written on a Macintosh.

Contents

Introduction

Two capsule biographies, one less often told:

José Raúl Capablanca y Graupera was born in Havana, Cuba, in 1888.

José learned chess at age 4 by observing his father's games. A popular legend goes that little José pointed out his father's incorrect knight move, and when his elders asked, "Oh? Just what do you know?", the boy showed them by beating his dad in his very first game.

The elder Capablanca took José to the Havana Chess Club, where the youngster was soon defeating all the adults. In 1901, at age 13, José won a 12-game match against Cuban champion Juan Corzo. After that, Capablanca concentrated on his schoolwork, until a 1909 match with Frank Marshall, in which he routed the American champion 8-1 with 14 draws.

Not every participant at the international San Sebastián tournament of 1911 believed Capablanca deserved entry, but the young Cuban won the tournament. He even won the brilliancy prize against Dr. Ossip Bernstein, one of the objectors.

Capablanca went on to compile one of the most spectacular tournament and match records in chess history. He suffered the fewest losses of any grandmaster — between 1916 and 1923, Capablanca did not lose a single tournament or match game, including the 1921 world championship match against Emanuel Lasker, who was No. 1 for 27 years.

Capablanca's air of invincibility — plus his rapid calculation at the board and a seeming effortlessness and clarity in his moves — earned him the nickname, "the human chess machine." Mikhail Botvinnik, who was world champion for 15 years, said he thought Capablanca displayed the greatest natural talent at chess. This natural ability contributed to Capablanca's self-admitted laziness: a fanatically hard-working Alexander Alekhine took the title in 1927.

The deposed champion played some of the best chess of his life while trying to secure a rematch with Alekhine, but one never took place. Even as late as 1939 — three years before Capablanca's death — Alekhine was declining offers for a rematch. The 1939 Chess Olympiad was Capablanca's last tournament, at which he won a gold medal. Alekhine — representing France — avoided Capablanca until the end, sitting out the France vs. Cuba Olympiad match.

Botvinnik also said: "You cannot play chess unless you have studied [Capablanca's] games." Capablanca was one of the game's finest teachers by example, but for textbook instruction, there was none better than Cecil Purdy.

Born in Egypt in 1906, then raised in Australia, Cecil John Seddon Purdy didn't learn chess until he was 16, but after just a year of practice, he was determined to be a chess writer.

Purdy's notebooks from the early 1920s included prospective titles like "Method of Thinking in Chess" and "Chess Made Easy," seeds for instructive books and articles that would move the American world champion Bobby Fischer to call Purdy "the best chess teacher in the business."

If Capablanca was "The Chess Machine," then Purdy was "The Technical Writer." While Capablanca's playing style was celebrated for its orderliness, Purdy's gift was an ability to distill a master game to its elements, and explain how those parts fit together.

Purdy published and edited magazines — *Australasian Chess Review, Check, Chessworld* — that served improving chessplayers from 1929 to 1967, providing pithy and memorable advice on every phase of the game, while recommending study habits and thinking patterns. Purdy followed his own counsel well enough to win the first world championship of correspondence chess, and the Australian over-the-board championship four times.

The purpose of this book is to make the case that Capablanca — the intuitive prodigy — and Purdy — the methodic educator — were teaching the same things.

At the very heart of winning chess, Purdy broke it down to two things, one positional and one tactical.

Threats are the basis of winning chess.

Threats are the lifeblood of a chess game, Purdy also said. Threats drive a chess game forward — if neither side makes a threat, a game of chess will only end through boredom.

A chessplayer is rarely as comfortable at the board as when his opponent's move is a quiet, non-threatening move. Ideally, a chess move should be as menacing as possible while developing one's forces.

Whether one is attacking or defending, the goal is to do so while bringing up unused pieces and pawns. According to Purdy:

The root principle of position play right through the game from opening to ending is: Use inactive force.

Superior force conquers. In *The Art of War*, Sun Tzu said: "The art of using troops is ... when [greater] his strength, attack him. ... A small force is but booty for one more powerful."

Maybe Purdy was referring to the Chinese military strategist here: "Can a force be inactive? In a military sense, yes, of course. In the chess opening, nearly all one's forces are inactive, so it's there the principle works most clearly; we call it development."

Those axioms about threatening moves and using inactive force pertain to every position we'll ever see on the board. Above the board, Purdy looks inside a chessplayer's head:

The chief factor in chess skill is the storing of patterns in the mind, and the recognition of such patterns in actual play.

Introduction

When a chessplayer sits at the board with steam coming from his ears, face red and pulling his hair out, it's because he doesn't know what to do.

But when a chessplayer has seen the position before, he can proceed with confidence. If the structures or piece configurations are in the player's memory, he doesn't have to reinvent the wheel — he can search his memory for the kind of move that worked before.

Checkmating patterns are the most valuable motifs a chessplayer can know. After a player learns the rules, and how the pieces move, the next thing he learns is often one of the simplest checkmating procedures — like the double rook roller or king plus queen vs. king.

The more checkmating methods the player recognizes, the more games he is able to win. In 1953, the authors Renaud and Kahn categorized and demonstrated many different checkmating themes in *The Art of the Checkmate*. The present book shows that Capablanca — legendary for his immediate sight of the board and recognition of the correct plan — finished some of his brightest games with the same checkmates described in *The Art of the Checkmate*.

Capablanca strived for efficiency, partly because he was lazy ("if businessmen gave as little time to their business as I generally give to chess, they would all go bankrupt in a very short time," he said). He looked for the shortest routes to winning chess games, and often that meant playing for mate.

By compiling an anthology of Capablanca's games that end in checkmate, it is hoped that a gap in chess literature will be filled. Capablanca is widely considered the greatest endgame player ever, and chess author Irving Chernev sought to instruct players in the queening of a pawn in his 1978 book *Capablanca's Best Chess Endings*. But a successful ending at chess can come about in two ways — pawn promotion or checkmate — and this book picks up Capablanca's instructive endgame play where Chernev's book left off.

Part I

The Art of the Checkmate

Genius ill-trained will not reach its utmost power; give it its proper development and you have... Capablanca.
— Julius du Mont

Chapter 1

What to Learn

Chessplayers buy a huge number of chess books, but read an incredibly small percentage of the books they purchase. A chessplayer will buy the Brooklyn Bridge if he thinks that will improve his play, but then he won't bother to cross.

If we were to recommend a course of reading for the chessplayer, we must keep in mind that most chessplayers either don't want to work hard, or don't have much time for study.

Checkmating Patterns

Checkmating patterns are the easiest things to learn, and the most profitable things to apply.

Logically speaking, you cannot win unless you can construct a checkmate, and it should follow that the more checkmates you can build, the more games you can win (and the more losses you can avoid).

The sports metaphors are numerous, and even appropriate. It's the successful golfers who make the putts, winning basketball teams who rise in the last two minutes, championship baseball teams who can close in the ninth inning. A proficient chessplayer must know how to deliver checkmate.

We are never lacking for a plan if we know some checkmating patterns. No matter which position is in front of us on the board, we can envision the checkmate that is closest to it, and aim for that. (The world champion Vasily Smyslov made many plans in that fashion: imagining the best squares for his pieces, and just moving them there.)

For inexpert players, openings books are most unhelpful. But once a student understands the tactical mechanics of Fool's Mate — 1. g4 e5 2. f3 ♕h4# — he can smartly navigate many openings. For instance, the Fool's Mate pattern inspires an excellent move in the Caro-Kann: 1. e4 c6 2. d4 d5 3. ♗d3 ♘f6 4. e5 ♘fd7 5. e6!, while 1. f4 e5 2. fxe5 d6 3. exd6 ♗xd6 threatens mate in three in answer to Bird's Opening.

Knowing various checkmating patterns aids in planning our opening, middlegame, and ending. So if our study time for chess were limited, that time is best spent learning checkmating patterns — because it helps in each phase.

An outstanding first book for anyone is *Bobby Fischer Teaches Chess*, which shows how the pieces move, guides the reader through the three ways of getting out of check, and most thoroughly covers the back-rank checkmating pattern.

Some enterprising chess educator should teach the other checkmating patterns in the same extensive fashion that *Bobby Fischer Teaches Chess* varies on the back-rank theme.

Until then, the best we can read are *The Art of the Checkmate* by Renaud and Kahn, and *How to Beat Your Dad at Chess* by Murray Chandler. (*The Art of the Checkmate* is in the old-fashioned descriptive chess notation — it pays to be multi-lingual.)

In this miniature, White's move 15 is easy to find if we have read *Bobby Fischer Teaches Chess*:

Game 1

London 1913
White: J.R. Capablanca
Black: F. Dunkelsbuhler
Petroff's Defense

1.	e4	e5
2.	♘f3	♘f6
3.	♘xe5	d6
4.	♘f3	♘xe4
5.	d4	d5

Because the black knight occupies the center, it does not control the center, and therefore e4 and d5 are susceptible to White's attack.

6.	♗d3	♗e7

Black opted for a less active bishop development because 6...♗d6 leaves d5 helpless.

7.	0-0	0-0
8.	c4	c6
9.	♘c3	...

If now 9...♘f6, Black is two moves behind in development with a lesser stance in the center.

9.	...	f5

Black strains to maintain his forward knight, but the light squares are further weakened, especially along the a2-g8 diagonal.

10.	cxd5	cxd5
11.	♕b3	...

Threatening to capture on d5 and also on e4.

11.	...	♘xc3
12.	bxc3	...

A materially-equal exchange favors the side whose pieces come forward with the recapture. 12. bxc3 brings up an unused unit, and the pawn might continue to c4 in coordinated effort against d5.

12.	...	♘c6
13.	♖e1	♗f6?

This book stresses two most elemental instructions: use inactive force, and examine all threatening moves. 13...♗f6 is a weak move because it does not activate an unused piece, and enables White to develop with a threat.

14.	♗a3	♖f7

Black didn't want to admit his error by retreating the bishop to e7.

15.	♕xd5!	1-0

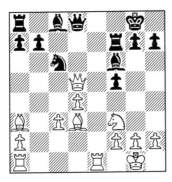

If 15...♕xd5, then 16. ♖e8+ ♖f8 17. ♖xf8# exploits the back rank. On other moves, 16. ♗c4 results in a decisive gain of material.

Elementary Methods for Pawn Promotion

When there is not enough force on the chessboard to engineer a checkmate, promote a pawn. One must know the elements of pawn endings, and how to handle the pieces in the endgame (in one word: actively).

For 50 years, Reuben Fine's *Basic Chess Endings* was called a bible, but it was a lot to chew. Some preferred Averbakh's *Chess Endings: Essential Knowledge or Practical Chess Endings* by either Keres or Chernev (same title, different books, both good).

Bruce Pandolfini gets a bad rap for producing commercial chess books, but his endgame book *Pandolfini's Endgame Course* is a good one, in which he devotes one page to each critical position and gives every one of them a name (for folks who more easily learn things with a pithy tag).

For many players, the technical endgames demonstrated in these books are mechanical and unexciting. Those players won't progress past an 1800 rating, but they probably don't mind.

Basic Textbooks

A sincere student should master the material in one beginner's book. (If one is very determined, read a different beginner's book every year, like world champion Mikhail Tal did.) Books like *Lasker's Manual of Chess*, Capablanca's *Chess Fundamentals* and *A Primer of Chess*, Fine's *Chess the Easy Way*, and Purdy's *Guide to Good Chess* are enduring classics.

In the last decade, it became good marketing practice to call readers stupid. I contributed to the second editions of Jim Eade's *Chess for Dummies* and Patrick Wolff's *The Complete Idiot's Guide to Chess*, both of which would have been useful without my help, while neither actually treated its readers as dumb or complete idiots.

All such books represent what masters believe to be a solid foundation of chess knowledge. Therefore, while I am suggesting five types of chess literature, the content overlaps from one type of book to another, especially in these general treatises.

Every generation has its chessplayers who are seduced by Aron Nimzowitsch's *My System*. The truth is that it isn't his system, but his peculiar choice of words to describe chess principles. One will find that the arcana described by Nimzowitsch is laid out in every other basic chess textbook, but in more common terms.

Please, please, if you choose to read Capablanca's *Chess Fundamentals*, avoid the McKay edition edited by grandmaster Nick de Firmian, who inexplicably purged several of Capablanca's games while appending modern games of no greater instructional value. I've long admired

15

de Firmian, a handsome local grandmaster, but what he did to Capablanca's book was wrong.

Games Collections

Writers learn by reading great books, painters learn by looking at masterpieces, and chessplayers learn by playing over the games of chess masters.

In fact, if done the right way, playing over master games is the best way to practice chess, more beneficial than playing chess. That's a hard thing to swallow: Playing chess is fun, but it doesn't help you get much better at chess.

The best chess practice was described by Purdy: With a chessboard, chess clock (set to a tournament time control) and scoresheet at hand, play through a master's winning games by covering the master's moves, playing a move on your own, then uncovering the master's move. Sometimes you guess right, yay. Sometimes you guess wrong, then retract your move while replacing it with the master move. By asking yourself why the moves are different, you will eventually grow to think like the master.

Purdy wrote: "A great mistake many players make is to feel disheartened if they don't understand fully every game they play over. If you understand some of a game, you are the gainer, and gradually you will find yourself understanding bigger slices."

It's vital to do this exercise with logical master games one can understand. A good chess teacher can suggest some — "nobody can learn how to play well merely from the study of a book," said Capablanca, "it can only serve as a guide and the rest must be done by the teacher if the student has

one; if not, the student must [learn] by long and bitter experience."

When I was an 1800-level player, I spent two years carrying *The Life and Games of Mikhail Tal*, because everyone — me, you, everyone — wants to be Tal. But the supernatural qualities that earned Tal the nicknames "magician" and "wizard" are exclusively Tal's. It's hard to say if I learned anything in two years of guessing Tal's moves.

The right player for everyone to study at the start is Paul Morphy, the first American champion. Morphy had a straightforward approach that sometimes resulted in fireworks — the thing to learn was that the brilliancies stemmed from proper positional play: whenever possible, making a developing move that threatened something.

After one learns Morphy, it's usually suggested that one move on to 1920s champion Capablanca, 1960s champion Fischer, or 1970s champion Anatoly Karpov, each of whom descended stylistically from Morphy.

One should hope to find a master to study whose manner of play is closest to one's own — the way to find that master takes time, going through many games to find the master whose moves one most often guesses correctly. The pitfall to this process is that if one does it before one is a good player, one will guess about 40 percent for everybody. So it's not a bad idea to stick to Morphy and Capablanca for a while.

There are many anthologies to study. Best for the recommended practice are collections annotated by the player himself — because only he knows what he was thinking — or annotated in an instructive manner.

Purdy used to recommend for this practice Chernev's *Logical Chess,*

Move by Move, which Chernev followed with *The Most Instructive Games of Chess Ever Played*.

Richard Réti's *Masters of the Chessboard* is another good book for the student, in which Réti explains positional concepts while introducing readers to great players of the early 20th century.

Max Euwe's *Chess Master vs. Chess Amateur* is an instructive book because each game demonstrates how a master takes advantage of amateur mistakes, the kinds we amateurs see most often.

Many players have read *Morphy's Games of Chess* by Philip Sergeant, but Sergeant's notes didn't seem didactic in nature. *A First Book of Morphy* — which was the best book I could write at the time, if not the blockbuster I had hoped to write — was meant to provide a set of instructive Morphy games.

Capablanca's Hundred Best Games by Harry Golombek was probably the most important book in my education as a chessplayer because they were Capablanca's games laid out with Golombek's helpful exposition. (Capablanca's notes to his own games suffered because he didn't like to write, and also because he withheld some information for thinking that his readers already knew it.) Grandmaster John Nunn thought as highly of Golombek's book as I, and Nunn's updated edition of Golombek's book is the best.

Fischer's *My 60 Memorable Games* is considered by many — patzers and grandmasters alike — to be the best chess book ever written. Fischer's games were the best of his time, while his notes and choice of games were not at all self-serving. No other chess master included lost games in an autobiographical games collection.

In these digital times, students don't have to cover the master's moves with a 3x5 card. Most chess software includes training features that ask one to guess moves, and any game reading application enables one to guess, then click.

Tactics

Ultimately, you're only as good as your tactical ability.

Games between non-masters are almost always determined by a one- or two-move tactic plus an "oops, I didn't see that." Luckily, there are countless tactics workbooks out there designed to improve one's chessboard vision.

Tactics books never (and endgame books rarely) go obsolete, but openings books quickly turn to rubbish. GM Larry Christiansen said *Reinfeld's 1000 Brilliant Combinations and Sacrifices* made him the fearsome attacker that he is, but you never hear a master credit an openings book with making him a better player.

The easiest chess puzzle books include problems that involve very few pieces, or where the pieces are laid out in a pattern that points one toward the right answer. It never hurts — and can always help — players of any level to work with the simplest tactical puzzles!

Some books include tactics puzzles that are torturously difficult. There is disagreement about how students should tackle such problems. Some players like the idea of sweating over one position for hours, while some think that if you don't see the answer in a couple minutes, you'll never see it. They think you should skip to the answer and learn it, so that when a similar position arises later in the book or over the board, you'll have a chance of going right.

I think getting through 100 puzzles swiftly — by knowing or by peeking — is more useful than slogging through a few slowly.

Capablanca-Cintrón, San Juan 1934, fits here as well as anywhere else in the book, a lesson in threats and tactics against an opponent who might've thought himself clever for a sophisticated openings choice and a weird little middlegame maneuver.

Game 2

San Juan 1934
White: J.R. Capablanca
Black: R. Cintrón
Sicilian Defense

1. e4   c5

There are couple of tales related to 1. e4 c5 in the Capablanca legend.

The first is that Capablanca shunned the Sicilian Defense because "Black's position is full of holes," which he is quoted as saying in Coles's 1956 book *Dynamic Chess*. No source earlier than that has been found for the quote, but it goes repeated

because it seems like something Capablanca would have said, considering his rare use of the defense, and his routs against it.

2. ♘e2   ...

The second story is from Fine in *The Chess Correspondent*, May-June 1942:

"Capa was a perfect example of the intuitive type of master, who sees that a move is good, but cannot explain why. I recall a story told to me by a strong amateur in Mexico, whom Capa once offered to teach. The gentleman was overjoyed and promptly appeared the next day for his lesson.

"'In the Sicilian Defense,' Capa explained, 'after 1. e4 c5 the best move is 2. ♘e2.'

"'Why?'

"'*No importa*, it does not matter; it is the best move.'

"And that was about all that the poor amateur could find out; it was the best move and that was all there was to it. Capa's judgment was usually right, so this absolute certainty in himself was an invaluable asset."

2. ...   ♘c6
3. d4   ...

It's shocking how many little kids and their chess teachers play 2. ♘f3 and 3. d4 against a Sicilian move order with no clue as to why.

It is about time and space. For 1. e4 c5, it helps to know a little bit about the Asian game Go (the operative words are "little bit" — how can anyone enjoy such a difficult game?). 1. e4 is like a stone at the 4,4 point in the lower right, staking a claim to the space in that quadrant. 1...c5 is like a stone at 3,4 — a slightly smaller space — in upper left.

From a chess perspective, both sides have stepped up to the fourth rank, while Black approaches the center from the wing. After 2. ♘e2 (2. ♘e2 and 2. ♘f3 differ in that White can push his f-pawn with no need of d2-d4 plus ♘xd4, while Black can't take a lead in development like he can against Alapin's Opening 1. e4 e5 2. ♘e2) ♘c6 3. d4 cxd4 4. ♘xd4, Black's space — from the viewpoint of the Go board or the chessboard — has vanished.

Also, White gains a unit of time because his knight has moved forward with the recapture. In other words, White sacrificed a more valuable center pawn for a wing pawn, but gained a bit of time plus a bit of space.

3. ...	cxd4
4. ♘xd4	e6
5. ♘b5	...

The threat of 6. ♘d6+ presses Black immediately — Fischer used to continue 5...d6 6. ♗f4 — but White risks losing time if the knight retreats to a3 or tangles his queen knight's development. Non-threatening developing moves like 5. ♘c3 and 5. ♗e3 are acceptable.

5. ...	d6
6. c4	...

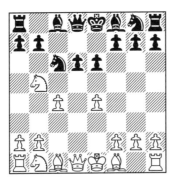

White controls d5, the square in front of Black's backward pawn, while the c4-pawn inhibits Black's queenside expansion ...b7-b5, and c2 is open for the knight in case White chooses ♘b5-a3-c2-e3 (for a stronger hold on d5).

6. ...	a6
7. ♘5c3	♘f6
8. ♗e2	♗e7
9. 0-0	♕c7
10. ♗e3	0-0
11. ♘d2	b6

In the 1980s, these "hedgehog" positions were very popular. If White overreaches, Black's position has flexible quills that can poke from many places.

12. ♖c1	...

Developing with a threat. Amateur Sicilian games unfold like this — Black plays moves that look masterly, but as soon as threats arise, the pretense crumbles.

12. ...	♖d8
13. ♘d5	♕b7

13...exd5 14. cxd5 also wins at least a pawn with a better position.

14. ♘xb6	♖b8
15. b3	...

There is no need to rush to 15. ♘xc8 because the bishop isn't going anywhere. Maybe if Black played ...♗d7 White would take it then, because Black's recapture would not gain time.

15. ...	♘d7
16. ♘xd7	...

Perhaps White opted to swap the lesser minor because the knight could be more immediately active.

16. ...	&xd7
17. ♘b1	...

A tidy regrouping. The queen may develop to coordinate with the dark-squared bishop and keep her eye on the d-file, while the knight can head back out to c3, and the f-pawn stays unblocked.

17. ...	&e8

Offbeat. Black wants to move his bishop to f6 while his d6-pawn is guarded, and then move ...♘e7, but e5 is usually the right square for a black knight in such positions.

18. ♕d2	&f6
19. ♖fd1	♘e7
20. f3	&c6
21. ♕a5	...

White looked around for threats to make, and saw that ♕a5 prepares c4-c5 with a discovery against a6, or &g5 as a skewer.

21. ...	♘c8?

It takes some kids years to learn that declaring oneself a Sicilian defender doesn't make one a chessplayer, but gaining tactical awareness does.

22. e5!	&h4

23. exd6	♘xd6

Black had to worry about 24. c5, securing the monster pawn on d6 while discovering against a6.

24. &f4	...

Now Black is defenseless against c4-c5.

24. ...	♕a7+
25. c5	♘b7
26. &xb8	1-0

Miniatures

The value of miniature games is incalculable. If there is a pattern to share, it can be demonstrated quickly with short games, which are easier to remember and more to the point than longer games.

Some people cluck their tongues because miniatures are always decided by some tactical goof, but they ought to understand that their opponents make the same goofs, so it behooves them to learn how to spot these and crush them.

Chernev compiled the classic *1000 Best Short Games of Chess*, and in the six decades since that was published, Nunn produced *101 Brilliant Chess Miniatures*, Burgess did *The Quickest Chess Victories of All Time*, and the American club player Bill Wall made a series of books grouped by opening.

Game 3

Budapest 1929
White: J.R. Capablanca
Black: Edgar Colle
Nimzo-Indian Defense

1. d4	♘f6

2.	c4	e6
3.	♘c3	♗b4
4.	♕b3	...

Capablanca didn't always play his invention 4. ♕c2, but when Black takes on c3, any difference in Spielmann's 4. ♕b3 becomes moot.

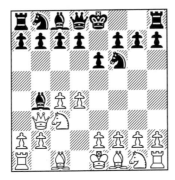

4.	...	♗xc3+
5.	♕xc3	♘e4
6.	♕c2	d5
7.	♘f3	0-0
8.	e3	♘c6

In his next chance at this position, Colle played 8...b6.

| 9. | ♗e2 | ♖e8 |
| 10. | 0-0 | e5? |

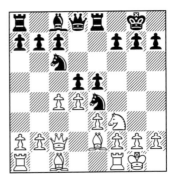

| 11. | cxd5 | 1-0 |

Black will lose a piece. If 11...♕xd5, then 12. ♗c4 attacks the guard. These things happen to masters like Colle, and they happen to club players all the time. To land on the right side of these accidents, one has to study tactics puzzles at home, and examine every threatening move at the board.

The following chapters about checkmating patterns follow the order and naming conventions from *The Art of the Checkmate*.

Parts 1 and 2 in *The Art of the Checkmate* were named "Picturesque Checkmates" and "Typical Checkmates" — the checkmates in this book are organized the same way; only the names of Parts 1 and 2 are changed.

Chapter 2

Légal's Pseudo-Sacrifice

Kermur de Légal was a pivotal figure in chess history. The best player in France in the early 1700s, de Légal taught Philidor, whose 1749 book *L'Analyze des Échecs* laid the foundation for modern chess theory.

Game 4

Paris 1750
White: Kermur de Légal
Black: St. Brie
Philidor's Defense

1.	e4	e5
2.	♘f3	d6
3.	♗c4	♗g4

Chess teachers call this the "bad pin," enabling White to plan his play around the unprotected bishop. When your opponent has one or more pieces exposed, look for a combination — a series of forcing moves based on a double attack.

4.	♘c3	g6?
5.	♘xe5!	...

One threat is 6. ♕xg4.

5.	...	♗xd1
6.	♗xf7+	♔e7
7.	♘d5#	1-0

Game 5

New York 1907
White: A. Pulvermacher
Black: J.R. Capablanca
King's Gambit Declined

1.	e4	e5
2.	f4	...

It's helpful to understand this difference between the King's Gambit — 1. e4 e5 2. f4 — and the Queen's Gambit — 1. d4 d5 2. c4. Both gambits aim to improve White's center control by deflecting or capturing the Black center pawn (note that 2. c4 does more to aid White's development than 2. f4). In the Queen's Gambit, 1. d4 d5 2. c4 dxc4 3. e4 or 1. d4 d5 2. c4 ♘f6? 3. cxd5 ♘xd5 4. e4 gives White some advantage, but in the King's Gambit, 1. e4 e5 2. f4 exf4 3. d4? is bad because

3...♕h4+ 4. g3 fxg3 threatens a powerful discovered check, while 1. e4 e5 2. f4 ♘c6 3. fxe5 is an unreal threat because 3...♕h4+ 4. g3 ♕xe4+ forks.

One of the bases for this book is that one cannot be a good chessplayer until one can recognize an unreal threat, then ignore it: 1. e4 e5 2. f4, and Black need not react to 3. fxe5 because it is an unreal threat. All that said, one's experience in chess is incomplete without a love affair with the King's Gambit.

2. ...   ♗c5

Because 3. fxe5 is an unreal threat, Black is at liberty to do as he likes. 2...♗c5 develops the bishop actively before ...d6 shuts it in.

3. ♘f3   ...

This move makes 4. fxe5 a genuine threat.

3. ...   d6
4. c3   ...

An important move. If White can achieve d2-d4, he'll claim the center while attacking the bishop. The gambit 4. b4 ♗xb4 5. c3 is admirable, but White has made too many pawn moves, while the weakness on the g1-a7 diagonal became evident in Jaffe-Reshevsky, New York 1920: 5...♗c5 6. d4 exd4 7. cxd4 ♗b6 8. ♗c4 ♘f6 9. ♕d3 0-0 10. 0-0 ♖e8 11. ♘bd2 g6 12. f5 d5 13. exd5 (White can ignore the threat: 13. fxg6 dxc4 14. gxf7+ ♔xf7 15. ♘xc4 is a promising sacrifice) ♗xf5 14. ♕b3 ♘g4 15. d6 ♖e3! 16. ♗xf7+ ♔g7 17. ♕c4 ♗d3 0-1.

4. ...   ♗g4

Fighting for control of d4, but White too easily breaks the pin.

5. fxe5   dxe5
6. ♕a4+   ♘d7

The threatening move 6...♗d7 is played most often. Then 7. ♕c2 ♘c6 8. b4 ♗d6 9. b5 ♘ce7 10. d4, and White's aim is achieved. It would seem that 5. fxe5 plus 6. ♕a4+ puts 4...♗g4 under a theoretical cloud, but at chess, theory is to practice as fantasy is to reality.

7. ♘xe5   ♘f6
8. d4   ...

Better than 8. ♘xg4, which brings the black pieces forward: 8...♘xg4 9. d4 (9. ♗e2 ♕h4+ 10. g3 ♗f2+ with advantage) ♕f6 10. ♕c2 0-0-0 11. dxc5? ♖he8 is a winning attack for Black.

8. ...   0-0
9. ♗g5?   ...

The difference of one tempo is huge, because 9. ♘xg4 is good: 9...♘xg4 10. ♗e2 ♕h4+ 11. g3, and then 11...♗f2+ is out of the picture. Instead, 9. ♗g5 is the "bad pin."

9. ...   ♘xe5!
10. dxe5   ...

Black's pieces are also swarming after 10. dxc5 ♘d3+.

10. ...   ♘xe4
0-1

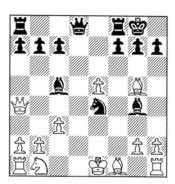

White resigned in view of 11. ♗xd8 ♗f2#, 11. ♕xe4 ♕d1#, and 11. ♕c2 ♕d1+! 12. ♕xd1 ♗f2#.

Chapter 3

The Power of the Double Check

A check may be answered by moving the king, capturing the checking piece, or interposing between the checking piece and the king (unless the checking piece is a knight).

In the case of double check, it can only be answered by moving the king, which makes possible some powerful trickery.

Game 6

New Orleans 1855
White: Judge A.B. Meek
Black: A.N. Other
King's Gambit

1. e4 ...

Judge Meek lost several games to Morphy, but he's also remembered for winning this one.

1.	...	e5
2.	f4	exf4
3.	♘f3	d5
4.	♘c3	...

Some sources identify Black as "Abdor," but give the gamescore as 4. exd5 ♕xd5 5. ♘c3 ♕d8 6. ♘e4 ♗g4 7. ♕e2 ♗xf3 8. ♘f6#, which makes no sense (why would White play 6. ♘e4, unless as a recapture?).

4.	...	dxe4
5.	♘xe4	♗g4
6.	♕e2	♗xf3?
7.	♘f6#	1-0

The double check means that both checking pieces are *en prise*, but immune to capture and unable to interpose.

Game 7

Kiev 1914
Simultaneous exhibition
White: J.R. Capablanca
Black: Masyutin
Staunton Gambit

1. d4 ...

This game is significant in my education as a chessplayer. In that most effective way of practicing chess — covering a master's moves and guessing them while replaying the game — it's most helpful to study a master with a classical approach, or whose style is close to one's own.

Before I discovered Capablanca-Masyutin, I was determined to be the next David Bronstein — the most artful grandmaster — but when my teacher asked me to guess at a Bronstein game of similar length, I guessed an unacceptable number of the moves correctly. On Capablanca-Masyutin, I did much better.

1. ...   f5

Like the hugely popular Sicilian — 1. e4 c5 — the Dutch Defense approaches the center from the direction opposite White's, and immediately unbalances the position, but the Dutch move does nothing to aid Black's development and exposes his king. "What a delight! I love playing against the Dutch," said world champion Tigran Petrosian.

2. e4   ...

In the Havana 1913 tournament book, Capablanca wrote that the Staunton Gambit 2. e4 is White's best answer to the Dutch Defense.

2. ...   fxe4

2...d6 might be tried, and if Black solves the problem of a backward e-pawn, he can get a good game.

3. ♘c3   ...

The immediate effect of 2. e4 fxe4 is that White is enabled to make three consecutive moves to threaten e4.

3. ...   ♘f6
4. ♗g5   ...

Threatening 5. ♗xf6 plus ♘xe4, but that threat is greater than its execution. "Once the threat is carried into effect, it exists no longer, and your opponent can devote his attention to his own schemes," said Capablanca.

4. ...   c6

An unnecessary pawn move. White has also won a good number of brilliancies after the more common 4...e6.

5. f3   ...

White's conquest of the center by 6. fxe4 is a strong positional threat, persuading Black to lose time with another capture. 5...d5 6. fxe4 dxe4 7. ♗c4 is a mess for Black.

5. ...   exf3
6. ♘xf3   e6

Had Black played this at move 4, he could now play ...♗e7 and ...0-0.

7. ♗d3   d5
8. 0-0   ...

Three extra moves in development usually justifies a pawn sacrifice in the opening. Black's excessive pawn moves mean that White has four moves to show for the gambit pawn.

8. ...   ♘bd7

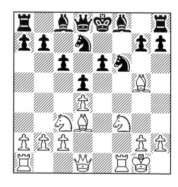

9. ♘e5   ...

The goal is to introduce the queen with a threat, but the f6-knight — reinforced by the d7-knight — prevents ♕h5+. 9. ♘e5 opens the queen's diagonal to h5, while White presses on the knights in three directions: ♘xd7,

♗xf6, and ♖xf6. 9. ♕e2 is a threat that can be ignored: 9...♗e7 10. ♕xe6 ♘c5.

9. ...   ♗e7

Not 9...♘xe5, because 10. dxe5 h6 11. ♗g6+ is very bad for Black, but for breaking the pin on the f6-knight, Black threatens to swap White's best-placed piece by 10...♘xe5.

10. ♗xf6   ♗xf6

A stronger defense is 10...♘xf6, and then White will have to be more inventive than 11. ♖xf6 ♗xf6 12. ♕h5+ g6 13. ♗xg6+ hxg6 14. ♕xg6+ ♔e7 15. ♕f7+ ♔d6 16. ♘c4+ dxc4 17. ♘e4+ ♔d5 18. ♘xf6+ ♔d6 19. ♘e4+ ♔d5 20. ♘c3+, where White could claim a draw.

11. ♕h5+   ♔e7

White is well ahead following 11...g6 12. ♗xg6+ hxg6 13. ♕xg6+ ♔e7 14. ♖xf6. The key to the position after 11...♔e7 12. ♕f7+ is that Black is chased into a burrow — 12...♔d6-c7-b8 — but if Black can be persuaded to move the d7-knight, the seventh rank is unblocked.

12. ♗xh7!   ...

An exceptional psychological move. 13. ♘g6+ is a bluff, but Black can't resist the move that prevents that fork while attacking the pinned bishop on h7!

12. ...   ♘f8
13. ♕f7+   ♔d6
14. ♘c4+!   ...

The first knight sacrifice that must be accepted. Black played 12...♘f8, so 14...♔c7 is impossible.

14. ...   dxc4
15. ♘e4+   ♔d5
16. ♖f5+   ...

Forcing the king to the e-file so that inactive force can be used.

16. ...   ♔xe4
17. ♖e1+   ♔xd4
18. c3+   ...

For many years, in every position, I could hear an old chess teacher's voice inside my head asking what I could do to bring up more new force. When I finally started doing it consistently, the voice disappeared, and I was so relieved.

18. ...   ♔d3
19. ♖d5#   1-0

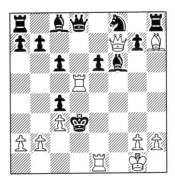

The double check is the only checkmating move. The h7-bishop neatly covers c2. Capablanca probably envisioned the whole king hunt at 12. ♗xh7!, even though he was busy playing against a crowd.

Game 8

La Habana 1913
White: Juan Corzo
Black: J.R. Capablanca
Old Indian Defense

1. d4   ♘f6
2. c4   d6

Two weeks earlier in New York, Capablanca played the Old Indian against Kline "with the idea of taking the game out of the usual lines ... now nearly every player is familiar with it." He wrote that in 1920, and by the 1950s, the King's Indian move 2...g6 had almost completely superseded the Old Indian (because the dynamic potential of the bishop on g7 was judged to trump the possible weakness of d6).

3.	♘c3	♘bd7
4.	e4	e5
5.	f4	...

Of doubtful value, said Capablanca. 5. f4 overreaches in the center and neglects White's development. White has an advantage in center control — compare the c- and d-pawns — his next job is mobilizing his pieces. White has the advantage after the modest 5. ♘f3 c6 6. ♗e2 ♗e7.

5.	...	exd4

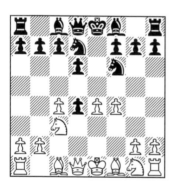

Necessary, said Capablanca, before White played 6. ♘f3 or 6. fxe5 to leave Black with a very bad game. As usual, he left the rest for the student to work out. 6. ♘f3 would have renewed the threat to e5, after which 6...exf4 is unacceptable for bringing up a white piece and capturing away from

the center, while 6...exd4 7. ♘xd4 is a more significant gain of time for White than ♕xd4 because knights need more time than queens to reach the other side of the board.

6.	♕xd4	♘c5
7.	♗e3	♕e7

Black blocks his bishop, but develops with a threat. The bishop is better on g7, anyway, where the white queen is in its sights.

8.	♘d5	♘xd5
9.	exd5	♗f5

Anticipating 10. 0-0-0 g6, after which 11. ♕xh8? ♕xe3+ is more effective because the white king is cut off. Then 12. ♖d2 ♕e1+ 13. ♖d1 ♕e4 is winning for Black.

10.	♘f3	g6
11.	♔f2	...

The unpin also guards the bishop, so 12. ♕xh8 is a more serious threat.

11.	...	♖g8
12.	♖e1	♗g7
13.	♕d1	...

Black must be vigilant. Even though White is in retreat, he threatens 14. ♗xc5.

13.	...	♘e4+
14.	♔g1	♔f8

According to Capablanca, 14... 0-0-0 exposes Black to attack. Black avoided, for instance, 15. ♗xa7 ♗xb2 16. ♗d3 ♖ge8 17. ♕b3 ♗g7 18. ♖b1 b6 19. ♗xb6.

15.	♗d4	g5!

Threatening 16...gxf4 to gain a pawn while unleashing the rook.

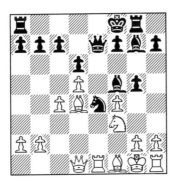

16. ♗xg7+ ...

Most lovely is the queen sacrifice plus double checkmate — 16. fxg5 ♘xg5 17. ♖xe7 ♘h3+ 18. gxh3 ♗xd4# — but White played a logical defense. First he opened d4 for an attacking knight move, then he kept the g-file closed.

16. ...   ♖xg7
17. ♘d4   ♗d7
18. f5   ...

Besides preventing the opening of the g-file, 18. f5 also stops Black from playing ...f5, so 19. ♗d3 is threatened.

18. ...   ♕e5

Capablanca gave the alternative 18...c5 19. dxc6 bxc6, enabling Black to maintain the knight with ...d5.

19. ♕d3   ...

The only threatening development White could make that keeps the knight protected.

19. ...   ♖e8
20. ♘e6+   fxe6
21. fxe6   ...

21. ...   ♖xe6!

A startling move. After the mundane 21...♕xb2 22. ♕xe4, the d7-bishop and e8-rook are shut out.

22. dxe6   ♗c6

If White could pass now, Black wouldn't have a threat, so he would make one with 23...♖e7. White could then develop his bishop — 24. ♕e3 ♖xe6 25. ♗d3 (25. ♕xa7? b6 seals off the queen, threatening 26...♕d4+ with a winning attack) — but his king rook would still be buried.

23. ♕f3+   ♕f4

24. ♕e3   ...

Remarkably, the side that's behind in material offers to trade queens.

Black's lead in mobility leads to a winning position in Capablanca's notes: 24. ♕xf4+ gxf4 25. h4 (Black is also ahead after 25. ♗e2 ♘f6) 25...f3 26. ♖d1 f2+ 27. ♔h2 ♘g3 28. ♖d2 (28. ♖d4 is much better, preventing 28...♖g4, and snuffing Capablanca's idea 28...♘xh1 29. ♔xh1 ♖xg2 because of 30. ♖f4+) 28...♘xh1 29. ♔xh1 ♖xg2!.

24. ...	♔e7
25. b4	b6
26. b5	♗b7
27. g3	♘d2
28. ♕c3	...

Capablanca recommended 28. ♗g2 instead. The endgame following 28. gxf4 gxf4+ 29. ♔f2 fxe3+ 30. ♔xe3 ♗xh1 31. ♔xd2 is better for Black.

| 28. ... | ♘f3+ |
| 29. ♔f2 | ♕f8 |

White missed this when he played 28. ♕c3, the champion wrote.

| 30. c5 | ... |

30. ♖d1 ♘e5+ 31. ♔g1 ♕a8 is a winning coordination of queen and bishop in an unusual setting.

30. ...	♘e5+
31. ♔g1	♘f3+
32. ♔f2	bxc5

Less perilous than 32...♘xe1+ 33. ♔xe1 ♗xh1 34. cxd6+ cxd6 35. ♕c7+ ♔xe6 36. ♗h3+ ♔f6 37. ♕c3+ ♔g6, even though Black is winning.

| 33. ♕a5 | ... |

Unable to break into c7 by cxd6+ plus ♕c7+, White spends additional time, and his counterplay comes up very short.

33. ...	♘e5+
34. ♔g1	♕f3
35. ♕xc7+	♔f6
36. ♕xd6	♕xh1+
37. ♔f2	♕xh2+
0-1	

Chapter 4

The Smothered Mate

A chess author wrote long ago that the classic smothered mate pattern is responsible for introducing countless students to the artistic possibilities of chess, by demonstrating the power of the double check (Renaud and Kahn knew what they were doing by putting the double check and smothered mate sections together in *The Art of the Checkmate*), showing a queen sacrifice, and ending with a demonstration of the knight's exclusive hopping ability.

1. ♕d5+   ♔h8

1...♕e6 is a useless interposition, while 1...♔f8 2. ♕f7# deprives the world of art.

2. ♘f7+   ♔g8
3. ♘h6+   ...

The great power of the double check requires that the king move out of check. Neither capture nor interposition is sufficient to escape.

3. ...   ♔h8
4. ♕g8+   ...

This is a hard one to sell to children who start crying the moment their queens leave the chessboard.

4. ...   ♖xg8
5. ♘f7#   1-0

Game 9

Karlsbad 1929
White: J.R. Capablanca
Black: Herman Mattison
Nimzo-Indian Defense

1. d4   ...

For the first 200 years of chess theory as we know it, controlling the center was mostly a matter of its occupation.

1. ...   ♘f6

Observes two center squares from a short distance with a developing move.

2. c4   ...

2. e4 was prevented, so White takes the broadest center stance possible.

2. ...   e6

2...e6 takes another little bite of the center while freeing the king's

31

bishop. Black preserves several options — 3...b6 is a Queen's Indian, 3...c5 is a Benoni, 3...d5 is an ordinary Queen's Gambit.

3. ♘c3   ...

Developing in readiness for 4. e4.

3. ...   ♗b4

Nimzowitsch, for whom this opening is named, was at the head of the hypermodern school of chess thought, which offered that controlling the center from a distance was just as valid as the classical theory of direct occupation. The Nimzowitsch defense to the queen pawn stands as the best the hypermoderns had to offer. Consider how Black's action fits in with this most general recipe for winning a chess game: Get better center control. Get better development. Get better king safety. Then from that superior position, attack the enemy king by opening files for your major pieces. Each of Black's moves influenced the center, but none stepped right in — by pinning the c3-knight, Black indirectly increased his pressure on e4 — while Black developed his kingside pieces as rapidly as possible in order to castle.

4. ♕c2   ...

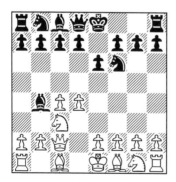

The logic behind Capablanca's trademarked move against the Nimzo-Indian is clear. The queen joins directly in the fight to control e4, while in case of ...♗xc3+, White can recapture with a piece move rather than double his pawns with bxc3. Chessplayers are notorious slaves to fashion — when some grandmasters in the 1980s realized "hey, 4. ♕c2 is the right way to go," every chessplayer suddenly took it up.

4. ...   c5

One drawback to 4. ♕c2 is that the d4-pawn is temporarily undefended. 4...c5 attacks it with a move that is consistent with the hypermodern notion of central control from outside the center.

5. dxc5   ...

A drawback of 4...c5 is that White's capture exposes the d7-pawn as backward. 5. dxc5 opens the line to the weak d-pawn, while Black's recapture does not gain time. Black would be happier if his bishop were not yet moved from f8.

5. ...   ♘c6

With 5...♘a6, Black can head for recapture on c5 with a forward-going move, but 6. a3 forces 6...♗xc3+ 7. ♕xc3 ♘xc5 8. b4, when White stands well on the queenside.

6. ♘f3   ♗xc5
7. ♗f4   ...

A more pertinent move is 7. ♗g5, though the bishop has more scope on f4. The critical center square in this position is d5, because until the d7-pawn reaches d5, it has no support from a neighboring pawn. 7. ♗g5 acts like Black's 3...♝b4, helping White control a key center square by pinning an enemy knight. However, one fascinating aspect of Capablanca's play was how his pieces just happened to be placed ideally when the key moments arose — the bishop will play a huge role on f4.

7. ...   d5

Naturally. It is O.K. to castle.

8. e3   ♛a5

When White played e2-e3, it cut the dark-squared bishop off from the queenside. Black hopes to exploit the dark squares on the queenside first with ...♛a5, then by replaying the bishop to b4, and maybe ...♞e4.

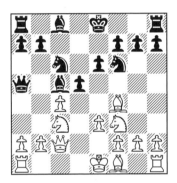

9. ♝e2   ...

In 1988, grandmaster Vladimir Bagirov thought to play 9. a3, so that if 9...♝b4, White would gain time with 10. ♖c1.

9. ...   ♝b4
10. 0-0   ...

White played moves 9 and 10 with a cool disregard for Black's plans about the dark squares.

10. ...   ♝xc3
11. bxc3   ...

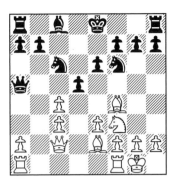

11. ...   0-0

If Black immediately targets c3 with 11...♞e4, White moves the pawn with 12. cxd5 exd5 13. c4, when White has better center pawns, a lead in development, and greater king safety. A slightly better alternative is 11...dxc4 12. ♝xc4 ♛c5 13. ♝d3 ♞d5, but White is still favored in terms of development and king safety.

12. ♖ab1   ...

It is this rook move and the next that gave this game its charm and instructive quality: Each white piece moves once before the fighting starts. 12. ♖ab1 ties the c8-bishop to the defense of b7, and foreshadows ♖b5.

12. ...   ♛a3

Black's first discernible goof, which threatens nothing, develops nothing, and lines up queen and rook for a bishop fork (the f4-bishop is magically placed).

13. ♖fd1   b6
14. cxd5   ♞xd5

White wins at least a pawn after 14...exd5 15. c4.

15. ♞g5   f5

Not 15...♞f6 because of 16. ♝d6, but 15...g6 keeps Black's shield closer to his body, and would save the c8-bishop from being stuck to the e6-pawn. For instance, 15...g6 16. ♗f3 ♗b7.

16. ♗f3   ...

Threatening 17. c4 ♘db4 18. ♕d2, with 19. ♗d6 to follow.

16. ...   ♕c5
17. c4   ♘db4

In case of 17...♘xf4, 18. ♖b5! ♕e7 19. ♗xc6 is a pretty in-between sequence, after which White captures on f4 or a8.

18. ♕b3   e5

Otherwise 19. ♗d6 is a killer.

19. a3   ♘a6
20. ♗xc6   ♕xc6
21. c5+   1-0

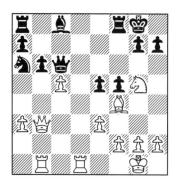

White finishes by smothering: 21...♔h8 22. ♘f7+ ♔g8 23. ♘h6+ ♔h8 24. ♕g8+ ♖xg8 25. ♘f7#.

Game 10

New York 1916
White: Christoph Schroeder
Black: J.R. Capablanca
Two Knights' Defense

1. e4   e5

2. ♘f3   ♘c6

About the immediate counter-attack 2...♘f6, Capablanca wrote that "[the Petroff Defense] is considered by the majority of experts to be slightly inferior to [2...♘c6]." Until improving players join the expert ranks, however, they should practice attacking whenever possible.

3. ♗c4   ♘f6

3...♗c5 is equally good, avoiding the complexities arising from White's 4. ♘g5.

4. ♘g5   ...

4. d4 is not as greatly confrontational, at least not immediately. The most popular move among modern masters is 4. d3, which is uneducated of a student, pretentious of club players.

4. ...   d5

Whereas 3...♗c5 was the safer move then, ignoring White's threat with 4...♗c5 is the boldest move now.

5. exd5   ♘a5

5...♘d4 and 5...b5 are tricky and worth exploring. 5...♘xd5 is a well-known mistake, reopening the bishop's line toward f7.

6. ♗b5+   ...

The alternative is Morphy's move 6. d3, freeing the queen's bishop, when an eventual ...♘xc4 dxc4 brings White forward.

6. ...   c6

Better than 6...♗d7. The d5-pawn has to be wiped out for reasons of center control, and to give the a5-knight a way home.

7. dxc6   bxc6

Black has to attack to justify his pawn sacrifice. 7...♘xc6 threatens nothing, and self-pins.

8. ♗e2   ...

The retreat 8. ♗a4 exposes the bishop to a possible fork: 8...h6 9. ♘f3 e4 10. ♘e5 ♕d4, while 8. ♕f3 ♖b8 shows White has moved his queen too early.

8. ...   h6

Driving the knight either to f3, where it can be attacked again, or to h3, where it is out of play.

9. ♘f3   e4
10. ♘e5   ♕c7
11. f4   ...

11. d4 exd3 12. ♘xd3 is O.K., but 11. f4 keeps the center pawn.

11. ...   exf3
12. ♘xf3   ♗d6
13. d4   0-0
14. c4?   ...

14. 0-0 is an equal game, where Black has good piece activity to compensate for the material deficit.

14. ...   ♘g4

It's no longer safe for White to castle kingside, and queenside is doubtful.

15. ♕d3   ...

15. ♕a4 looks like an improvement, taking the queen off a fork at f2, and aiming at the exposed knight. Then Black should keep developing with 15...♖e8 rather than play the materialistic 15...♘xh2, enabling White to develop with a threat by 16. ♗d2.

15. ...   ♖e8

Not distracted by the h2-pawn, Black brings up new force.

16. ♘c3   ♗g3+!
17. hxg3   ...

17. ♔f1 ♘f2 is a little better.

17. ...   ♕xg3+
18. ♔d2   ♘f2

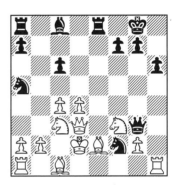

19. ♖h3   ...

The prettiest finish is 19. ♕c2 (19. ♕b1 ♘xc4+ 20. ♗xc4 ♕f4+ 21. ♔c2 ♗f5+ wins) ♘xc4+ 20. ♔e1 ♘d3+ 21. ♔d1 ♕e1+ 22. ♖xe1 ♘f2#.

19. ...   ♗xh3
0-1

Game 11

Barcelona 1920
White: J.R. Capablanca
Black: Coll
Colle System

1. d4   d5
2. e3   ♘f6
3. ♗d3

In *How to Think Ahead in Chess*, I.A. Horowitz recommended this move order to reach the Stonewall Attack —

where White continues 4. f4 plus 5. ♘f3 — but if that's what White had in mind, Black's misplay causes him to change course.

3. ...   ♗g4

A mistake, enabling White to gain time with f3.

4. ♘e2   e6
5. 0-0   ♗e7
6. ♘d2   ...

A pawn is better suited to c3 than the knight, as it supports the center in case of ...c7-c5 and inhibits ...♘c6-b4.

6. ...   0-0
7. f3   ♗h5

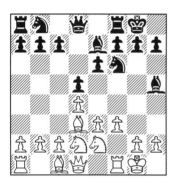

8. e4   dxe4

White can't make the ideal recapture 9. fxe4 because of 9...♗xe2 10. ♕xe2 ♕xd4+. However, compare this position to a typical Colle: 1. d4 d5 2. ♘f3 ♘f6 3. e3 ♗g4 4. ♗d3 e6 5. 0-0 ♗e7 6. ♘bd2 0-0, where White can't afford 7. e4 dxe4 8. ♘xe4 ♗xf3 9. ♕xf3 ♕xd4. In the game at hand, since White could play 8. e4, it is clear that he gained time.

9. ♘xe4   ♘d5

Perhaps Black was afraid of 10. ♘f4 ♗g6 11. ♘xg6, but he ought to

accept that, since 9...♘d5 is a further loss of time.

10. c3   c6

Another questionable move. Black should strive for ...c7-c5 in one step.

11. ♗d2   ...

White surely contemplated 11. ♘f4 ♘xf4 12. ♗xf4 as a more active way to develop the bishop, but for having played 10...c6, Black might not have been persuaded to move his knight.

11. ...   ♘d7
12. f4   ♗xe2?

A gross waste of time. If Black thought he had to make this trade, he should've made it at move 4. Black need not have been terrified of 13. ♘4g3 ♗g6 14. f5.

13. ♕xe2   ♖e8
14. ♖ae1   ...

How smoothly White's game progressed after the woeful 12...♗xe2.

14. ...   ♘5f6

14...♘7f6 is better. Black is playing poorly, but you must understand that your opponents are just as bad, so examples of strong players demolishing weak players are valuable. Euwe and Meiden's *Chess Master vs. Chess Amateur* is a whole book of such games.

Inexpert chessplayers delude themselves into thinking that they must out-maneuver their opponents as in a grandmaster game, but if the average player concentrates on using inactive force, and examining all the threatening moves, the wins will pile up.

15. ♘g5   h6

15...♘f8 and 15...♗d6 are both better.

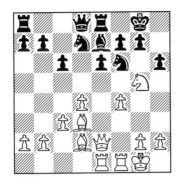

16. ♘xf7   ♛c7

16...♚xf7 17. ♛xe6+ ♚f8 18. ♗g6 wins.

17. ♛xe6   ♗f8
18. ♘xh6+ ♚h8
19. ♛g8+!   ♘xg8
20. ♘f7#   1-0

Chapter 5

The *Guéridon* and *Épaulettes* Mates

The most famous example of the *guéridon* checkmate is in Fischer's *My 60 Memorable Games*, maybe the best chess book ever.

Bled 1959
White: Paul Keres
Black: Bobby Fischer

52. ♔d5   g4

Keres saw he couldn't deal with the g-pawn, but rather than resign, he made the principled move to support his passed pawn's advance.

53. ♖c4   ♛e5#
0-1

That was a titanic struggle in which Keres sacrificed his queen in the opening against Fischer's favorite Najdorf

Sicilian. The checkmating pattern is called the *guéridon* — French for "pedestal" — because the piece configuration resembles a small table (the name "swallowtail mate" is seen occasionally).

Game 12

Frankfurt 1912
White: Walther von Holzhausen
Black: Siegbert Tarrasch
Two Knights' Defense

1.	e4	e5
2.	♘f3	♘c6
3.	♗c4	♘f6
4.	d4	exd4
5.	0-0	...

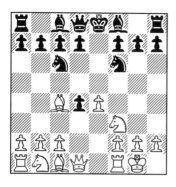

5. ...   d6

The main line 5...♘xe4 6. ♖e1 d5 7. ♗xd5 ♕xd5 8. ♘c3 is banal, which is part of the reason modern masters lean toward 4. d3.

6. ♘xd4   ♗e7
7. ♘c3   0-0
8. h3   ...

Because 8...♘e5 9. ♗b3 c5 10. ♘f3 ♗g4 is a bother.

8. ...   ♖e8
9. ♖e1   ♘d7?

Quite the boner by Tarrasch, who in 1914 would be named one of the original five grandmasters of chess. There are shorter examples to demonstrate the pattern, but none with Tarrasch's marquee quality.

10. ♗xf7+   ♔xf7
11. ♘e6!   ♔xe6
12. ♕d5+   ♔f6
13. ♕f5#   1-0

Game 13

Bahla Blanca 1911
White: J.R. Capablanca
Black: J. Vargas
Colle System

1. d4   d5

2. ♘f3   e6
3. e3   ♘f6
4. ♗d3   ♗d6

In theory, it is incorrect for Black to follow suit with this bishop development. White will play ♘bd2 plus e3-e4 (which will threaten a pawn fork) or c2(3)-c4, and then if Black is persuaded to capture ...dxe4 or ...dxc4, the knight's recapture will hit the bishop on d6. In practice, ...♗d6 works well if Black can maintain his bishop's active placement, especially if he can achieve ...e5 himself.

5. b3   ...

In the Zukertort flavor of the Colle System, White plays 0-0, ♘bd2, ♖e1, and then e3-e4 to free the bishop along c1-h6. Here White will use the bishop on two diagonals: c1-h6 and a1-h8.

5. ...   c6
6. ♘bd2   ♕e7
7. a3   ...

Preventing ...♗a3, which would reduce White's attacking forces while relieving Black's cramped position. To ease traffic jams on crowded freeways: don't build bigger roads, remove the cars.

7. ...   ♘bd7
8. ♗b2   ♘f8
9. ♘e5   ♘g6
10. f4   ♗xe5
11. fxe5   ♘e4
12. ♗xe4   ...

12. ♘xe4 dxe4 13. ♗xe4 ♕h4+ costs a piece. White can see his surprise at move 17 coming, else he probably would have played 12. 0-0.

12. ...   dxe4
13. ♘xe4   ♕h4+
14. ♘f2   ♕g5

15.	0-0	♕xe3
16.	♗c1	♕c3

The only safe square for the queen. Black was most pleased to threaten the rook, but White ignored the threat.

17.	♘e4!	♕xa1
18.	♘d6+	♔f8

White wins the queen on 18...♔d8 19. ♗g5+. That theme recurs on 18...♔d7 19. ♖xf7+ ♘e7 20. ♖xe7+.

19.	♖xf7+	♔g8
20.	♕f1	...

Threatening 21. ♖f8+ ♘xf8 22. ♕f7# or 21. ♖xg7+ ♔xg7 22. ♕f7#.

20.	...	♕xd4+
21.	♔h1	h6
22.	♖xg7+	1-0

22...♔xg7 23. ♕f7 is the *guéridon* mate.

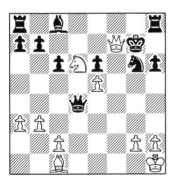

Game 14

Moscow 1935
White: J.R. Capablanca
Black: Grigoriy Levenfish
Semi-Slav Defense

1.	d4	d5
2.	c4	c6

The Slav Defense was invented so that Black could maintain a pawn on d5, but without blocking the c8-bishop.

3.	♘f3	♘f6
4.	e3	...

4. ♘c3 further tempts Black to play 4...dxc4, and then in anticipation of 5...b5, White can play most enterprisingly with 5. e4, or surround the c4-pawn with 5. a4.

4.	...	e6

In these Semi-Slav positions, the c6-pawn's first job is to maintain the center, and then after the e6-pawn assumes that role, its second is to aid an expansion on the queenside. It's stuff for masters, but it's amazing how many club players can recite theory with no understanding of the practice. I wasted years as one of those players — I used to know the Polugaevsky Sicilian better than Polugaevsky, but as soon as I had to invent a move on my own, I would lose. Below the 2200 level, many more games are determined by tactics than by the recitation of opening theory.

5.	♘c3	♘bd7
6.	♗d3	dxc4

Elsewhere in this book we see how 6...♗d6 7. 0-0 0-0 8. e4 dxe4 9. ♘xe4 ♘xe4 10. ♗xe4 ♘f6 11. ♗c2 leads to a promising position for White.

7.	♗xc4	b5
8.	♗d3	a6

The development 8...♗b7 9. 0-0 a6 10. e4 c5 is more sensible. Black never touched his queen's bishop in this game!

9.	e4	...

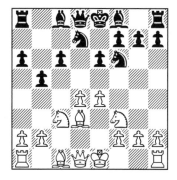

9. ...   c5

9...h6 was played in Seirawan-Diesen, Lone Pine 1977. The Lone Pine events were a benefaction for strong players, held in a Sierra Nevada paradise with no entry fees, but a rating floor that rose yearly. Yasser Seirawan and Mark Diesen were two of the best young Americans — both won the world junior championship — but Seirawan became a chess professional who doesn't play chess, while Diesen (d. 2008) got a real job. Playing chess is no way to make a living.

10. e5   ...

10. d5 is played almost as often, with an eye toward an endgame in which White has a passed pawn. But 10. e5, sacrificing a pawn, is immediately threatening.

10. ...   cxd4

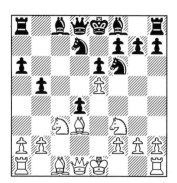

11. ♘xb5   ...

More popular than the centralizing 11. ♘e4 because 11. ♘xb5 loosens b5 for a threatening move by White's bishop.

11. ...   ♘xe5

If 11...axb5 12. exf6 gxf6 13. 0-0 ♕b6 14. ♕e2, then Black has a bunch of center pawns, but his development and king safety are lagging — an unclear and unbalanced position desirable to modern masters.

12. ♘xe5   axb5
13. ♕f3   ...

13. ♗xb5+ is played more often, but Capablanca chose the threatening move that introduced the greatest unused force.

13. ...   ♖a5

The threatening developing moves 13...♕a5+ and 13...♗b4+ are much better.

14. 0-0   b4
15. ♗f4   ...

15. ♖e1 introduces a bigger chunk, but when that rook develops to c1 instead, it carries the seeds of two threats.

15. ...   ♗e7
16. ♖fc1   0-0
17. ♕h3   ...

Not yet 17. ♘c6 because 17...♗b7 pins.

17. ...   ♖c5

If Black develops with 17...♗b7, then 18. ♘g4 threatens to remove the guard of h7, and to make a bishop fork on c7.

18. ♖xc5   ♗xc5

19. ♗g5 ...

A stronger threat than 19. ♖c1, which threatens to capture a bishop, while 19. ♗g5 threatens to remove a guard and then deliver checkmate.

19. ... h6
20. ♘g4 ♗e7
21. ♗xf6 ...

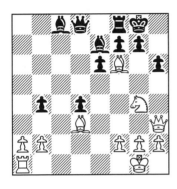

21. ♘xh6+ also leads to mate.

21. ... gxf6

Required knowledge: 21...♗xf6 22. ♘xh6+ gxh6 (22...♔h8 avoids mate, but Black is lost) 23. ♕xh6 ♖e8 24. ♗h7+ ♔h8 25. ♗g6+ ♔g8 26. ♕h7+ ♔f8 27. ♕xf7#.

22. ♘xh6+ ♔g7
23. ♕g4+ ♔h8

The *guéridon* checkmate is 23...♔xh6 24. ♕h4+ ♔g7 25. ♕h7#.

24. ♕h5 ♔g7
25. ♘xf7 ...

Threatens the *guéridon* 26. ♕h7#, while 25...♖xf7 26. ♕h7+ ♔f8 27. ♕h8 is also mate.

25. ... ♖h8
26. ♕g6+ 1-0

The Old Fork Trick

The "old fork trick" is an opening capture-plus-pawn-fork combination designed to gain control of the center.

Game 15

New York 1913
White: J.R. Capablanca
Black: H. Liebenstein
Three Knights' Game

1. e4 e5
2. ♘f3 ♘c6
3. ♘c3 ♗c5

3...♗c5 makes it too easy for White to take over the center. It's the kind of mistake you see in elementary-school chess classrooms, but Adolf Anderssen — perhaps the world's best player until Morphy showed up — gave it a whirl.

4. ♘xe5 ...

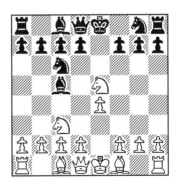

4. ... ♗xf2+

The trick is seen in 4...♘xe5 5. d4 ♗d6 6. dxe5 ♗xe5, when Black has lost time with his bishop and space in the center.

5. ♔xf2 ♘xe5
6. d4 ♘c6

There is much to learn from examples of good players exploiting weak play. Piškur beat Vertačnik in the 2001 Ljubljana Open by consistently introducing new force with threats: 6...♕h4+ 7. g3 ♕f6+ 8. ♔g2 ♘g6 9. ♗c4 (threatening a skewer with 10. ♖f1) 9...♕d8 10. ♖f1 f6 11. ♕h5 (threatening 12. ♗xg8) 11...♘e7 12. e5 (threatening 13. exf6 to vitalize the rook) 12...f5 13. ♗g5 (threatening 14. ♖xf5) 13...d6 14. ♖ae1 (threatening 15. exd6 to win the e7-knight) 1-0.

7. ♗e3 ...

Black threatened 7...♕f6+.

7. ... d6
8. ♗e2 ...

White didn't have time to develop the bishop more actively with 8. ♗c4 because 8...♘f6 9. ♖f1 ♘g4+ was bothersome.

8. ... ♘f6
9. ♖f1 0-0
10. ♔g1 h6

One of the drawbacks to ...♗xf2+ is that it opened a file for White's use. 11. ♗g5 would have been a painful pin.

11. ♕e1 ...

Lifting the queen up the d-file would not make for a threatening developing move, but ♕g3 will.

11. ... ♖e8
12. ♕g3 ♔h8
13. ♖f2 ...

14. ♖af1 will introduce White's last unused piece with the threat 15. ♗xh6.

13. ... ♕e7
14. ♗d3 ♘g4
15. ♘d5 ♕d7
16. ♖f4 ...

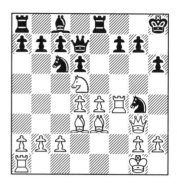

16. ... ♘d8

16...♘xe3 was Black's last chance to stay in the game.

17. ♖xg4 ♕xg4
18. ♘xc7 ...

Black lost time with 16...♘d8, and will lose more. While he is rounding up this knight, White can arrange the winning kingside attack.

18. ... ♕d7
19. ♘xa8 b6
20. d5 ♗b7
21. ♗d4 f6
22. ♕g6 ...

You will see the "desperado" move 22. ♘xb6 so often in positions like this, but White won this game by saving time, so why should he give some back?

22. ... ♗xa8
23. e5 ♔g8
24. exf6 1-0

Game 16

New York 1912
White: J.R. Capablanca
Black: Will Randolph
Three Knights' Game

1. e4 e5
2. ♘f3 ♘c6

3.	♘c3	♝c5
4.	♘xe5	♝xf2+
5.	♔xf2	♘xe5
6.	d4	♘g6

When Black played 3...♝c5, he set himself up for a bad position, but he had a genuine option here. 6...♘c6 threatens 7...♛f6+ with a fork, whereas 6...♘g6 is closer to the white king.

7.	♝c4	d6
8.	♖f1	...

8.	...	♝e6

A more forcing move order than 8...♘f6 9. ♔g1 ♝e6, when White can opt for 10. ♛d3 or 10. ♛e2, and the pin 11. ♝g5 is still in store.

9.	♝xe6	...

Because he omitted ...♘f6, Black ruled out 9. ♛e2 as then 9...♛f6+ forks.

9.	...	fxe6
10.	♔g1	♘f6
11.	♝g5	0-0
12.	♛d3	...

White has the advantage in central control and space, plus the mobility conferred by the bishop. But he will be willing to forgo one of those advantages in order to create threats.

12.	...	♛d7
13.	♝xf6	...

The result is a backward pawn on an open file while White controls the square in front of the backward pawn — a serious liability for Black.

13.	...	♖xf6
14.	♖xf6	gxf6
15.	♖f1	♖f8
16.	♛b5	c6

Black ought to prefer to sacrifice a pawn or two to gain activity for his rook, but there's a surprise at the end of 16...♛xb5 17. ♘xb5 a6 18. ♘xc7 ♖c8 19. ♘xe6 ♖xc2 20. ♖xf6 ♖xb2 — 21. h4 threatens 22. h5 to drive the knight off before 23. ♖f8#, a form of the Arabian Mate.

17.	♛b3	...

Black has been pressed into taking on another couple of weak pawns — his queen is tied to defending three — so he tries correcting them.

17.	...	d5
18.	exd5	cxd5
19.	♘e2	...

Maybe the knight will go to f4 to hit e6 and d5, or to h5 where it hits f6. Like 16. ♛b3, 19. ♘e2 is just a move White made while looking around for threats.

19.	...	♔g7
20.	c3	e5

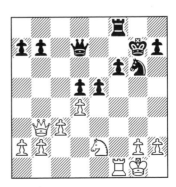

Black overdoes it. 20...e5 permanently weakens the d- and f-pawns. White hasn't made a concrete threat yet, so Black should probably be patient, and make some move that gives his queen more freedom — like 20... b6, so at least she's not tied to that pawn.

21. ♘g3   ♘e7

On 21...f5 22. dxe5 ♘xe5 23. ♕c2 ♔g6, Black has the royals plus a rook guarding one dumb pawn, and then 24. ♕e2 plus 25. ♕h5+ will make Black sorry he was so material-conscious. 21...♘f4 is best.

22. ♘h5+   ♔g6

It might get worse for Black if he abandons the f6-pawn: 22...♔h8 23 dxe5 exploits the pin.

23. ♕c2+   e4

23... ♔xh5 24. ♕xh7+ wins for White.

24. ♕e2   ...

Black should be thinking here, "If I lose the f-pawn, but manage to activate my pieces while tucking my king away, I will have some chances in the endgame based on my protected passed pawn. Or if I can get the queens off the board, then my exposed king will suddenly be an active fighting piece."

Black is also thinking, "I can't activate my rook with 24...♖g8 because 25. ♖xf6+ is ruinous, and I can't shelter my king with 24...h6 and 25...♔h7 because ♘xf6+ forks. The only threatening moves I can make are ...♕f5 and ...♕g4, which lose my queen for nothing. Wow, my position is bad."

24. ...   f5

Maybe this is the best Black can do, so that ...h7-h6 and ...♔h7 won't run into a fork, and if Black can achieve ... f5-f4, he can use f5 as a square for his pieces.

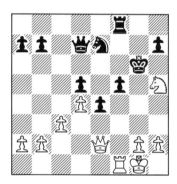

25. g4   ...

White doesn't have a true threat. If Black passes, then 26. gxf5+ ♖xf5 27. ♕g4+ ♔h6 28. ♕g7+ ♔xh5 29. ♕xh7+ is only sufficient to draw. But 25. g4 introduces new force, so if Black passes, then 26. ♔h1! threatens the above, and then after 28...♔xh5, 29. ♖g1! wins.

For that reason, 25. ♔h1 can be considered a better move — because it prepares 26. g4 as a genuine threatening move.

25. ...   h6

The best move is 25...♖f7, relieving the pin on the f5-pawn, so that 26. ♔h1 can be met by 26...fxg4.

26. gxf5+   ♖xf5
27. ♕g4+   ♖g5

Obviously, Black planned 27...♖g5, though checkmates don't get much prettier than the *guéridon*-like 27... ♔f7 28. ♕g7+ ♔e6 29. ♕f6+ ♖xf6 30. ♖xf6#.

28. ♖f6+   ♔h7

29. ♖f7+   ♔h8

Alternatively, 29...♔g6 30. ♖g7#, while 29...♔g8 30. ♖g7+ and 31. ♖xg5 wins a rook.

30. ♖f8+   ♘g8

White wins on 30...♔h7 31. ♕xg5 and 32. ♘f6+. Instead 30...♘g8 enables the same combination in a longer sequence.

31. ♕xg5   hxg5
32. ♖xg8+   1-0

The *Épaulettes* Mate

The *épaulettes* checkmate is a close relative of the *guéridon*.

Correspondence 1890
White: J.W. Showalter
Black: Logan

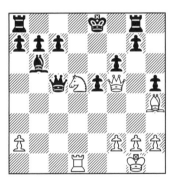

Jackson Whipps Showalter was U.S. champion five times in the late 1800s, but then came Pillsbury and Marshall, the best Americans after Morphy and before Fischer. Showalter played the "Capablanca freeing maneuver" on the Black side of the Queen's Gambit in 1897, when Capablanca was 9 years old.

22. ♕e6+   ♔f8
23. ♗xf6   ...

Bringing up the least active piece with a threat of mate in three.

23. ...   ♖e8

The rooks look like *épaulettes*, the giant ornamental ribbons that military officers wear on their shoulders. If 23...gxf6, White can engineer a winning discovered check: 24. ♕xf6+ ♔e8 25. ♕xe5+ ♔d7 (25...♔f7 26. ♕f6+ ♔e8 27. ♖e1+ leads to mate) 26. ♘xb6+.

24. ♘e7   ...

Threatening 25. ♘g6#. If Black's rook leaves the back rank, then ♖d8+ is a killer, but Black thinks he's worked out a defense.

24. ...   ♕xf2+
25. ♔h1   ♕xf6
26. ♘g6+!   ♕xg6
27. ♖f1+   ♗f2

In 1890, they transmitted moves by stagecoach, so Black's useless interpositions could have delayed checkmate long enough for White to die.

28. ♖xf2+   ♕f6
29. ♖xf6+   gxf6
30. ♕xf6#   1-0

Game 17

Moscow 1925
White: J.R. Capablanca
Black: Efim Bogoljubow
Queen's Gambit Accepted

1.	d4	d5
2.	c4	e6

If Black wants to accept, this is an inflexible sequence. After the usual 1. d4 d5 2. c4 dxc4, if White chooses the most direct 3. e4, then Black can hit back with 3...e5.

3.	Nf3	dxc4
4.	e4	c5
5.	♗xc4	cxd4
6.	♘xd4	♘f6

Compare to the modern line 1. d4 d5 2. c4 dxc4 3. e4 e5 4. ♘f3 exd4 5. ♗xc4 ♗b4+, where Black is freer.

7.	♘c3	...

7.	...	♗c5

In Hübner-Radulov, 1973 Leningrad Interzonal tournament, Black played 7...♘bd7 instead. Then 8. 0-0 ♗c5, and now the trademark Capablanca sacrifice doesn't work as well: 9. ♗xe6 ♗xd4, and because there is no bishop on e3, White cannot win a pawn by 10. ♗xd7+ ♕xd7 11. ♕xd4. White has some chances after 10.

♕xd4 fxe6 11. e5, but it's unsuitable for a tournament of such import.

The 1973 Leningrad Interzonal has a unique place in chess history: Karpov won, and was seeded into the world championship candidates' matches, which he also won, thus earning the right to challenge world champion Fischer in a match that — infamously — never took place.

8.	♗e3	♘bd7
9.	♗xe6!	...

Opening pawn sacrifices are made for reasons of mobility (controlling the center, leading in development, deflecting the the enemy queen) or safety (preventing castling, creating an attack). A piece sacrifice should combine and multiply the effects.

9.	...	fxe6
10.	♘xe6	♕a5

10...♕b6, forking, must be preferable here.

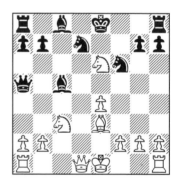

11.	0-0	...

It is imperative that White bring new forces to the game. 11. ♘xg7+ is impatient: 11...♔f7 12. ♘f5 and Black may develop; for instance 12...♘b6, threatening ...♘xe4.

11.	...	♗xe3

Black is aware that White's recapture activates the f1-rook for free, but he reasoned that while he is ahead in material he should exchange pieces, and he couldn't move his d7-knight (to mobilize the queenside) without losing the bishop on c5. Attempts to start the kingside are perilous: 11...♔f7 12. ♕b3, or 11...♔e7 12. ♘xc5 ♘xc5 13. ♘d5+.

12. fxe3   ...

A by-product of this capture is that White's threat of ♘xg7+ suddenly grows in significance. If the g7-pawn disappears now, White's pressure along the f-file stretches further than f6.

12. ...   ♔f7

13. ♘xg7+ isn't the only knight to fear. In case of 12...♖g8 (a miserable kind of move in any case), then 13. ♘b5 makes two threats: 14. ♘c7+ and 14. e5!.

13. ♕b3   ...

Threatening 14. ♘g5+ ♔g6 15. ♕f7+ ♔xg5 16. ♕xg7+ ♔h5 17. ♘d5, winning.

13. ...   ♔g6
14. ♖f5   ...

13. ♕b3 introduced new force with a threat, while making room for the a1-rook to improve. 14. ♖f5 introduced new force with a threat, while making room for the a1-rook to improve.

14. ...   ♕b6
15. ♘f4+   ♔h6
16. g4   g5

When Purdy first described his never-improved-upon training method — covering the winning master's moves and guessing them while play-

ing through the game — he said that if you guess a move incorrectly, look at the opponent's reply immediately, because it might suggest the reason for the right move. He also said that the annotator's comments would sometimes unravel the mystery. In this instance, the only thing the annotator has to say about 16. g4 is that it introduces new force with a threat, while Black's reply explains that the threat was 17. g5#.

However, 16. g4? is marked in the history books as a mistake. Capablanca wrote later that 16. ♕f7! will win. As I write this, I think I'll leave 16. ♕f7! for the student to work out, but award an "A" for effort if 16. g4 was guessed.

17. ♕xb6   axb6

18. ♖d1   ...

Sometimes the best you can do is to develop with a threat of a threat. White has in mind 19. ♖d6, which menaces the beautiful *épaulettes* mate 20. ♖dxf6+ ♘xf6 21. ♖xf6+ ♔g7 22. ♘h5+ ♔g8 23. ♘d5 h6 24. ♘e7+ ♔h7 25. ♖f7#.

18. ...   ♖g8

When behind in material, your best chance to get back into the game is to attack your opponent as hard as you can with the remaining material. So your opponent's winning method is to exchange as many of the potential counterattackers as possible. Black's best is to trade knights with 18...gxf4 19. g5+ ♔g7 20. gxf6+ ♘xf6.

19. ♘fd5   ♘xg4

Black can swap in this position, but it brings up a white piece. 19...♘xd5 20. ♘xd5 threatens 21. ♘e7, with initiative.

20. ♘e7   ♖g7

Black's thinking behind 18...♖g8 plus 20...♖g7 was that if 21. ♘xc8 ♖xc8, the g7-rook guards the d7-knight, but the drawback is that the rook limits his king's mobility.

21. ♖d6+   ♔h5
22. ♖f3   ♘gf6

Black needed a flight square.

23. ♖h3+   ♔g4
24. ♖g3+   ...

A neat time-gaining maneuver that confines the black king.

24. ...   ♔h5
25. ♘f5   ...

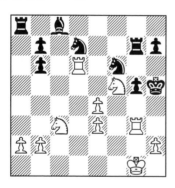

25. ...   ♖g6

On 25...♖g8, White can use inactive force: 26. ♖h3+ ♔g6 (26...♔g4

27. ♔g2! [threatening 28. ♘h6#] 27...♖g6 28. ♖xh7 ♘xh7 29. ♖xg6 with 30. h3+ next) 27. ♖h6+ ♔f7 28. e5 invites the e-pawn to the party.

26. ♘e7

Maybe White is repeating the position to gain time on the clock. 26. ♖h3+ ♔g4 27. ♔g2 effectively continues the attack.

26. ...   g4

Better is 26...♘c5, threatening to fork on e4.

27. ♘xg6   ♔xg6
28. ♖xg4+   ♔f7
29. ♖f4   ...

White transitions seamlessly from problem-like mating attack to efficient endgame play. After coordinating the rooks against the f6-knight, White can advance his passed pawn.

29. ...   ♔g7
30. e5   ♘e8

The other threatening move — 30...♘h5 — abandons the knight to 31. ♖f5.

31. ♖e6   ♘c7
32. ♖e7+   1-0

White adds to his material lead after 32...♔g6 33. e6.

Game 18

Barcelona 1929
White: J.R. Capablanca
Black: Edgar Colle
Symmetrical English

1. c4   ...

The greatly respected chess master and author John Watson devoted his career to promoting the English Opening, but it's hard to overlook what Andrew Soltis (another master/ writer) had to say, that English Opening players are "closet 1. d4 players."

In most Englishes, White strives to improve his center control with d2 (-d3)-d4, so only the move order has changed. And in cases where Black plays 1...e5 to make it a Reversed Sicilian, the key move for the Sicilian side is P-Q4 — in this case, d4 for White.

1.	...	♘f6
2.	♘f3	c5
3.	♘c3	♘c6
4.	d4	...

Keeping in mind what GM Soltis said, the rule of thumb about the Symmetrical English is that the first side to play P-Q4 gains some advantage.

4.	...	cxd4
5.	♘xd4	♘xd4?

A complete loss of a move, startlingly bad from a master. When chess educators introduce the principle of gaining or losing time with captures, they can start with the Center Game: 1. e4 e5 2. d4 exd4 3. ♕xd4 develops a white piece, but then 3...♘c6 gets the move right back.

Then they show the Scotch Game: 1. e4 e5 2. ♘f3 ♘c6 3. d4 exd4 4. ♘xd4, and then 4...♘xd4? is a mistake because 5. ♕xd4 develops a white piece when Black can't regain the time. The same applies to the Scotch Four Knights: 1. e4 e5 2. ♘f3 ♘c6 3. ♘c3 ♘f6 4. d4 exd4 5. ♘xd4 ♘xd4?, which is identical to this English position before us, except the c-pawns are advanced instead of the e-pawns.

6.	♕xd4	g6
7.	e4	d6
8.	♗e3	♗g7

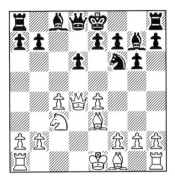

This could've been reached by a Sicilian move order: 1. e4 c5 2. ♘f3 d6 3. d4 cxd4 4. ♘xd4 g6 5. c4 ♘f6 6. ♘c3 ♘c6 7. ♗e3 ♘xd4? 8. ♕xd4 ♗g7, so the game might be used as evidence in Capablanca's case against the Sicilian.

9. f3 ...

A useful move in many ways. The black knight can neither leap to g4 to hit the e3-bishop, nor grab the e4-pawn when the c3-knight is pinned. If White launches a kingside pawn storm, f3 helps White achieve g2-g4. (The term "pawn storm" is so colorful — some students ask specifically how to create "pawn storms," and are disappointed to find that the goal is merely opening lines for the pieces.)

9. ... ♕a5
10. ♕d2

Black's diagonal coordination on c3 meant that a discovered attack by the f6-knight was more serious than before. Additionally, 10. ♕d2 unpins the c3-knight, while forming a queen-and-bishop battery for White.

10.	...	a6
11.	♗e2	♗e6
12.	♖c1	...

It looks curious to place the rook on a closed file, but 12. ♖c1 accomplishes much. White wants to play b2-b3 to bolster the c4-pawn, but that lengthens the g7-bishop's scope — so 12. ♖c1 moves the rook off the hot diagonal, while watching over the loosened c3-knight. Also, White looks ahead to ♘d5 to hit the backward pawn on e7, and if Black swaps on d5, then cxd5 will open the file for the rook. Finally, d1 is left vacant for the other rook.

12. ...   ♖c8
13. b3   ♘d7
14. 0-0   0-0

15. ♘d5   ...

This discovery is a common tactic in such positions, for instance, this miniature: 1. e4 c5 2. ♘f3 d6 3. d4 cxd4 4. ♕xd4 ♘c6 5. ♗b5 ♗d7 6. ♗xc6 ♗xc6 7. ♘c3 ♘f6 8. ♗g5 e6 9. 0-0-0 ♗e7 10. ♖he1 ♕a5 11. ♔b1 0-0 12. ♕d2, which aims mainly to centralize the f3-knight, but Black blundered with 12...♖ad8?, and resigned after 13. ♘d5.

15. ...   ♕d8
16. ♕b4   ...

Going where the threats are. There are other menacing moves, but 16. ♗g5 ♖e8 is no big deal, and Black can ignore 16. ♘f4.

16. ...   ♗xd5

If 16...b6, then White cannot pounce with 17. ♘xb6 because the

knight is pinned by 17...♖b8, but instead 17. ♖fd1 develops with the threat of 18. ♘xb6 ♖b8 19. c5!.

17. cxd5   ♖xc1
18. ♖xc1   ♕b8

To avoid material loss, Black conceded an additional rank of space to cxd5 and the only open to file to ♖xc1. To White's point of view, these gains are just as valuable.

19. ♕c4   ♗b2
20. ♖c2   ♗f6

19...♗b2 gained time on the clock. 20...♗f6 guards the e7-pawn from attack along the seventh rank.

21. f4   ...

A crafty little move. Black's knight is restricted, while White prepares to improve his light-squared bishop with a threat. Additionally, if White wins a pawn in the center, then his pawn majority is further along for that endgame ahead.

21. ...   ♖d8
22. ♕c7   ♕a8

Black hates the idea of simplifying the position with 22...♕xc7 23. ♖xc7 to improve White's rook, but a move like ...♕a8 is a clear admission that one's position is crumbling.

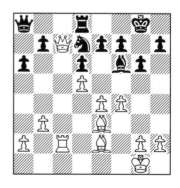

23. ♗g4	♘c5
24. e5	...

A clearer path than 24. ♗xc5 dxc5 25. ♖xc5, leaving bishops of opposite colors on the board, an endgame which is notoriously hard to win, but a middlegame that is sometimes shockingly easy. When an opposite-colored bishop takes part in a middlegame attack, it's as if the attacker is a piece ahead because the attacking bishop is unopposed, but in the ending the defender's opposite-colored bishop can make waiting moves and blockades that cannot be broken.

24. ...	♗g7
25. ♕xe7	h5
26. e6!	...

Ignoring Black's threat, while creating strong threats of his own.

26. ...	hxg4
27. exf7+	♔h7

27...♔h8 28. ♕h4+ ♗h6 29. ♕xh6# is unusual and pretty.

28. ♕h4+	♗h6
29. f5	g5
30. ♗xg5	♔g7
31. ♕xh6+	1-0

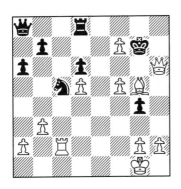

Every white piece is involved in 31...♔xf7 32. ♕h7+ ♔f8 33. ♗h6+ (imagine the bishop placing an *épaulette* on the black king's shoulder) ♔e8 34. ♖e2+.

Hübner's Blockading Plan

Grandmaster Nimzowitsch was an entertaining writer — his 1929 Karlsbad tournament book was very lively. Nimzowitsch's *My System* taught many people to play well, even though the ideas expressed didn't constitute a new system at all, but some well-accepted ideas wrapped in different paper.

One of the pithy instructions from *My System* concerned how to play against a weak pawn: "Restrain, blockade, destroy!", but who didn't already know that it's harder to hit a moving target?

White: Morris
Black: Hobbes
Nimzo-Indian Defense

1.	d4	♘f6
2.	c4	e6
3.	♘c3	♗b4
4.	a3	

White has a dozen reasonable choices after the Nimzo-Indian move 3...♗b4. Sämisch's 4. a3 forces ...♗xc3+, but Black usually plays that move whenever it doubles the c-pawns. Capablanca's 4. ♕c2 prevents the weakened c-pawns.

4.	...	♗xc3+
5.	bxc3	...

The old advice is "avoid doubled, isolated, and backward pawns" because such pawns are less mobile. The c3-pawn is immobile.

5. ...   c5

5...c5 is one black pawn that re-
strains two white pawns. White will
not further unhinge his pawns with
dxc5 when ...♕a5 or ...♘a6 regains the
pawn with structural advantage.

6. e3   0-0
7. ♗d3   d6
8. ♘e2   ♘c6
9. e4   ...

White's idea at move 4 was to resolve the queenside quickly, and then
build the pawn center.

9. ...   e5
10. d5   ♘a5
11. f3   ...

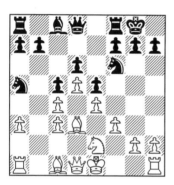

White has a huge pawn center, but
the c4- and e4-pawns are fixed on light
squares, frustrating the bishop on d3.
The center is restrained and blocked,
and Black can aim to destroy the c4-
pawn after ...b7-b6 plus ...♗c8-a6
(White's plan is to castle and play f3-
f4 — his kingside attack can be fierce).

The blockading scheme is named
for German grandmaster Hübner,
who enriched the idea decades after
its discovery — its most famous example was game 5 of the 1972 world
championship match between Fischer
and Spassky.

Game 19

Buenos Aires 1914
White: J.R. Capablanca
Black: A. Israel
Bird's Opening

1. f4   ...

Bronstein's *1953 Zurich International Chess Tournament* is a giant of
chess literature, disguising a stack of
positional teachings as a tournament
book. The first lesson Bronstein laid
down in that book was about the con-
nectedness of the chessboard: "The
point of an attack on the dark squares
is that by placing my pawns and pieces on the dark, I attack my opponent's
pieces and pawns on the light."

1. ...   d5
2. ♘f3   ♘f6
3. b3   e6
4. ♗b2   c5
5. e3   ♘c6
6. ♗b5   ...

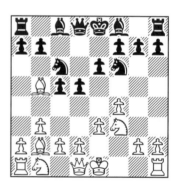

White's first six moves were sin-
gle-mindedly aimed at control of the
central dark squares — control that
will spread to the other color.

This light-squared bishop development fits so harmoniously with
White's scheme to dominate the dark
squares that Black would have liked to

prevent it with ...a7-a6, but that just results in his falling further back in development. White would develop the king's bishop elsewhere, and ...a7-a6 goes as a wasted move.

6. ...   ♗d7

Black's light-squared bishop is a problem. It's trapped behind a wall of pawns, and freeing the bishop with the advance ...e6-e5 is most unlikely, given White's stranglehold on the dark squares.

7. 0-0   a6

Black doesn't understand. White wants to swap the b5-bishop for the c6-knight because the knight contests the dark squares. The move ...a7-a6 is wasted effort, prompting White to make a move he wants to make anyway. It's like Sämisch's move against the Nimzo-Indian — 1. d4 ♞f6 2. c4 e6 3. ♞c3 ♝b4 4. a3 — where 4. a3 nudges Black to make his desired trade. Sämisch's idea was to resolve the queenside immediately, and then build a huge pawn center, but in Bird's Opening, Black has less time to take such a plan forward.

8. ♗xc6   ♗xc6

Black might think he did well to avoid doubled pawns on the c-file, but the bishop on c6 is not much better than a pawn.

9. c4   ...

White's lock on the dark squares is complete, so he gets to work on the other color. If Black's pawns were doubled on the c-file, then 9. c4 would be very strong for immobilizing two pawns. Black avoided that difficulty, but his improved mobility meant only that his pawn on b7 could move — an

insignificant gain in terms of center control and piece development.

9. ...   ♞d7

This would make a lot more sense if it were possible for Black to continue ...f7-f6, ...♝f8-d6, ...e6-e5.

10. ♞c3   ♛c7
11. ♖c1   f6

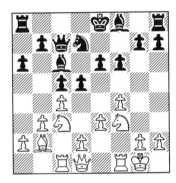

11. ♖c1 signaled cxd5 is coming to open the line for the rook, and when Black recaptures ...exd5, the e6-pawn vanishes. So Black is not playing ...f7-f6 to prepare ...e6-e5, he's playing it to block the diagonal so he can move his bishop without losing the g7-pawn.

12. cxd5   exd5
13. d4!   ...

A very good move. 11. ♖c1 developed the rook, then 12. cxd5 improved its sight. 13. d4 forces the removal of the c5-pawn, bettering the rook again, enabling the centralization of the f3-knight, and isolating the d5-pawn. Black can't play 13...c4 14 bxc4 dxc4 15. d5 ♝b5 16. a4, trapping the bishop, or 13...b6 14. dxc5 bxc5 15. ♞xd5.

13. ...   ♖d8

Black's king never found safety, but it's understandable that he avoided putting a second royal piece in line with the white rook by 13...0-0-0.

14. dxc5 ♘xc5
15. ♘d4 ...

The d5-pawn is the type that fomented Tartakover's saying, "an isolated pawn spreads gloom all over the chessboard." Isolated pawns have less mobility than healthy pawns partly because they have no friendly neighbors to jab at blockaders (here Black lacks a c- or an e-pawn to kick the knight on d4) or to assist their advance. The d5-pawn hinders the bishop on c6 and the rook on d8. Meanwhile, the white pieces are unhindered.

15. ... ♛f7

White was threatening to remove the guard by 16. b4, then fork with 17. ♘e6.

16. b4 ♘d7
17. b5 ...

Two straight threatening moves force this pawn swap, enabling White to bring his pieces up with threats. White's control of the dark squares made for easy posting of his knights, which are attacking light squares. It's one of those games where Capablanca made good chess look easy.

17. ... axb5
18. ♘cxb5 ...

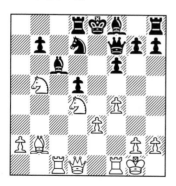

18. ... ♘b8

White was threatening the whimsical 19. ♘c7+ ♚e7 20. ♘f5#.

19. ♘e6 ...

A simple fork begets the royal fork if 19...♛xe6 20. ♘c7+.

19. ... ♗xb5
20. ♘c7+ ♚d7
21. ♘xb5 ...

22. ♖c7+ is menaced.

21. ... ♘c6
22. e4 ...

Instructions: Use inactive force, ideally to make threatening moves. To attack the enemy king, open files for the major pieces.

22. ... ♚c8
23. ♛a4 ♚b8
24. ♗d4 ...

More unused force comes to bear on the black king.

24. ... ♗d6

White was planning 25. ♗a7+ ♚c8 26. ♗b6 plus 27. ♛a8+ with checkmate to follow. 24...♗d6 enables interposition on b8.

25. e5! ...

The pawn plays a vital role in the mating attack! White could've leapt in with 25. ♗a7+, but instead used every unit. Botvinnik, a boxer before he was world chess champion, said he wanted to put all his might behind one punch to knock his opponent out. That was easier than throwing a jab, trading a few punches, skirmishing a bit, then retreating to the corner before the next round. Hit them one time with all your power, Botvinnik said.

25. ...	♗c7
26. ♖xc6	...

Fritz software can append inelegant comments to chess moves. About 26. ♖xc6, it might've said "demolition of king shield," but in this case, that would be pretty fitting.

26. ...	bxc6
27. e6	♕e7

The queen had to stay in touch with c7, else 28. ♕a7+ and 29. ♕xc7#.

28. ♕a7+	♔c8
29. ♕a8+	♗b8
30. ♕xc6+	♗c7
31. ♕a8+	♗b8

A lighter *épaulette* than usual.

32. ♖c1+	1-0

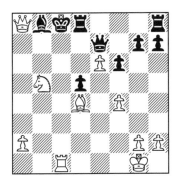

Game 20

Philadelphia 1918
White: J.R. Capablanca
Black: C. Haussmann
Bird's Opening

Nimzowitsch could have cited this game as an example of Capablanca as a hypermodern — relying more on surrounding the center than in direct occupation — but Capablanca believed in whatever worked, experimenting and winning with many openings.

1. f4	...

Bird's opening, controlling e5 from the side, is most promising if White can arrange a "Nimzo-Indian Defense in reverse."

1. ...	d5
2. ♘f3	e6
3. e3	c5
4. b3	...

Logical for the queen's bishop, so it can help control e5. If White brings about the ideal blockade, then ♗a3 will hit c5.

4. ...	♘f6
5. ♗b2	♗e7
6. ♗b5+	♘c6

6...♗d7, threatening, is better.

7. c4	...

Why didn't White didn't play 7. ♗xc6+ before Black could prepare to recapture on c6 with a piece? Some players prefer to recapture on c6 with the b-pawn because it moves toward the center, but that is shortsighted, not seeing difficulty with the immobile c-pawns.

7. ...	0-0

White didn't mind if Black played 7...♕c7, and Black didn't think it was important.

8. 0-0	a6

8...♕c7 was an improvement, even if 9. ♗xc6 ♕xc6 10. ♘e5 is an easy leap forward.

9. ♗xc6	bxc6
10. ♘e5	♗b7

A horrible thing to do to a bishop. Losing a pawn by 10...♗d6 11. ♘c6 ♕c7 was more considerate.

11. d3   ...

The hypermoderns like this c4-d3-e3-f4 pawn setup. The center squares are surrounded by pawns, and if the bishop's pawns are swapped, the recaptures go forward.

11. ...   ♘e8
12. ♘d2   f6
13. ♘g4   ♕c7
14. e4   ...

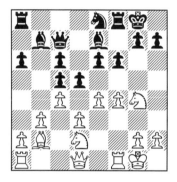

The desired blockade, where three pawns hold four.

14. ...   d4
15. ♕f3   ...

Pieces must go where the threats are. The queen is more mobile on the third rank than after 15. ♕e2, and following ♕g3, there is the possibility of ♘h6+, which might become a real threat.

15. ...   ♖d8

The b-file is the only useful file for a black rook — 15...♖b8 plus ...a6-a5-a4 gives some life to the rook and that sad bishop on b7.

16. ♕g3   f5
17. ♘f2   ...

The position is so locked up that White would prefer not to exchange a knight for a bishop after 17. ♘e5 ♗d6.

17. ...   g6

17...fxe4 18. ♘fxe4 trains the knight's sights right on c5.

18. e5   ...

The center is closed, so play will shift to the wings. Kasparov recommended looking at the board in halves divided at the d- and e-files to estimate attacking chances — White has more space east of the e-file, where his pieces are bigger.

18. ...   ♘g7
19. ♘h3   ...

There are dangers in every position, even those where the pieces sneak up gradually. 19. ♘f3 loses a pawn to 19...♘h5.

19. ...   ♘h5
20. ♕f3   h6

Probably a mistake. If White plays ♘g5, then Black's bishop is hardly worse after ...♗c8. But for playing ...h7-h6, the g6-pawn is weakened, and Black should see White's attack coming on the g-file.

21. ♔h1   ♔h7
22. ♖g1   ♖g8
23. g4   fxg4
24. ♖xg4   ♖g7
25. ♖ag1   ♕d7

It's easier for White to move pieces around the e4/e5 pawn wall. 25...♗f8 26. ♕g2 ♕f7 27. ♘e4 followed by 28. ♗a3 isn't much different.

26. ♘e4   ♕e8
27. ♗a3   ...

Finally, the ideal coordination against the c5-pawn. Black's queen becomes overworked.

27. ...   ♕f8

28.	🖢xg6	🖢xg6
29.	🖢xg6	♔xg6
30.	🖢g4+	♔h7
31.	🖢xh5	...

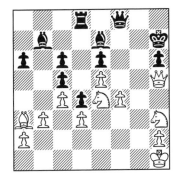

31.	...	🖢g7

Better is 31...♔g7 32. 🖢g4+ ♔h8 33. 🖢g6 🖢g7 34. 🖢xg7+ ♔xg7 35. ♗xc5 ♗xc5 36. ♘xc5 ♗c8 37. ♔g2 ♔f7 38. ♔f3 🖢g8, when the rook has no entry points on the g-file, but White's win isn't clear.

32.	♘hg5+	♗xg5
33.	♘xg5+	♔g8
34.	♘xe6	🖢d7
35.	🖢g6+	1-0

Chapter 6

Capablanca's Mate

When Renaud and Kahn set out in the early 1950s to categorize the various checkmating themes for the purposes of writing their wonderful book, they overlooked this checkmate arising in three games by the third chess champion of the world.

The rook gives check and covers the seventh rank, while the knight covers the potential flight squares on the eighth. After that, it is a matter of guarding the checking piece from capture.

Game 21

La Habana 1901, Match (8)
White: Juan Corzo
Black: J.R. Capablanca
Hamppe-Allgaier Gambit

1. e4 ...

When chess students grow ambitious enough to memorize games, the first one that many learn is Morphy-Duke of Brunswick and Count Isouard, Paris 1858 — because if it's not the single best game ever played, it's one of the most instructive. Which game do most students learn next? I don't know (I think chess teachers might agree that once a kid shows the dedication to do that first bit of work, then they can start working on collections and families of games). Corzo-Capablanca, 8th match game, was the second game I learned, and it was also one of the first games for which I wrote notes. In 2001, I annotated it again for the *California Chess Journal*, calling on everything I'd learned in 25 years. That piece won an award for analysis! But when I tackled the game a third time, I discovered how much I'd overlooked. This is attempt no. 4.

1. ... e5
2. ♘c3 ...

The Vienna Game can improve on the King's Gambit. If White plays 2. f4, the plan is to gain control of the center by deflecting the e5-pawn, or maybe capturing it. The problem for White is that 2. f4 doesn't truly threaten to take on e5 — if Black passed, and White played 3. fxe5 as planned, then Black gains the edge with 3...♕h4+.

Since 2. f4 is an unreal threat, Black can play as he likes, and he should march into the center with 2... d5. Black can also opt to accept the gambit by 2...exf4, and then White cannot grab the center with 3. d4 because 3...♕h4+ is still a stinger, so 3. ♘f3 prevents ...♕h4+, but again Black can hit the center with 3...d5. The Vienna move 2. ♘c3 inhibits ...d7-d5 in preparation for White's f2-f4 advance.

2. ...   ♘c6

2...♘f6 can bring about 3. f4 d5, which is a different game.

3. f4   ...

Another point to 2. ♘c3 is that it guards e4, so 4. fxe5 is a genuine threat here. That is, if White continues 4. fxe5, he gains advantage from 4...♕h4+ 5. g3 (because 5...♕xe4+ is prevented), or 4...♘xe5 5. d4.

3. ...   exf4

One of Fischer's best-remembered quotes pertaining to chess was, "You've got to give squares to get squares." White's pawn sacrifice permanently weakened the dark squares in his kingside (4...♕h4+ looms still), but Black has been deflected from the center. White's ideal is to achieve the d2-d4 advance, then recover the gambit pawn on f4, after which he would have the most desirable center pawn formation, while the f-file is open for his major pieces.

4. ♘f3   ...

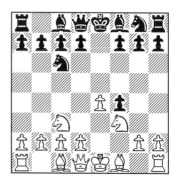

A sharp King's Gambit variation is the Bishop's Gambit: 1. e4 e5 2. f4 exf4 3. ♗c4 — inhibiting ...d5 and giving the king a safe flight square — so if Black leaps at 3...♕h4+, then White steps aside 4. ♔f1 and gains a move later with ♘f3. Black can threaten mate with 4...♗c5, but 5. d4 is White's answer. Here 4. ♗c4 is mistaken because of 4...♕h4+ 5. ♔f1 ♗c5, and then 6. d4 is out for the inclusion of ...♘c6.

4. ...   g5

The pawn on f4 is no ordinary pawn. White would especially like to play d2-d4 plus ♗xf4, restoring the material balance while claiming a better center, but as long as the f4-pawn stands, the c1-bishop is restrained and the a1-rook is stuck behind the bishop. After White castles kingside, the rook on f1 is also limited by the f4-pawn. Black wants to maintain that pawn because it bottles up White's pieces.

5. h4   ...

Applying the same positional logic, White wants to knock the f4-pawn down, so he aims at the rear of the pawn chain. A pawn chain is like a tall building — if you want to blow up a building, you put the explosives in the basement, not on the top floor. White has no time to waste — if 5. ♗c4 ♗g7 6. h4, then Black's rook is guarded after 6...h6 7. hxg5 hxg5.

5. ...   g4

Not 5...h6 because 6. hxg5 shows the h6-pawn to be pinned. Not 5...f6 because 6. ♘xg5 fxg5 7. ♕h5+, when a weak kingside diagonal leading to the enemy king is working in White's favor instead of Black's.

6. ♘g5   ...

White could build some pressure against f7 if he continues 7. ♗c4, but before that, Black can attack the knight while it has no safe retreat.

6. ...   h6
7. ♘xf7   ♔xf7
8. d4   ...

8. ♗c4+ appears most natural, but after 8...d5 9. ♘xd5, 9...♘a5 avoids trouble from a discovered check, while Black is relatively comfortable after 8. ♗c4+ d5 9. ♗xd5+ ♔g7 with ... ♘f6 coming. Another alternative — 8. ♕xg4 ♘f6 9. ♕xf4 — is obtuse.

8. ...   d5

The blow to the center threatens 9...dxe4, discovering against d4.

9. exd5   ...

9. ♘xd5 would enable 9...♘f6 as a threatening move. Khalifman's team said 9. ♗xf4 is best.

9. ...   ♕e7+
10. ♔f2   ...

A piece down, White doesn't want to play 10. ♕e2. In Game 6 of the match, Corzo self-pinned with 10. ♗e2, and the game was eventually drawn after 10...f3 11. gxf3 gxf3 12. 0-0 ♕xh4. Capablanca's story is that he overheard Corzo saying that White improves with 10. ♔f2, so the 13-year-old did some homework before Game 8.

10. ...   g3+
11. ♔g1   ♘xd4!
12. ♕xd4   ♕c5
13. ♘e2   ♕b6!

This is the move that makes the 11...♘xd4 combination special. 13... ♕xd4+ 14. ♘xd4 ♗c5 15. c3 is lifeless, but 13...♕b6 threatens 14...♗c5 and compels the exchange.

14. ♕xb6   axb6

A materially-even exchange favors the side whose pieces develop or improve as a result of the swap. 14... axb6 mobilizes the rook for free, while Black still threatens mate in two after 15...♗c5+.

15. ♘d4   ♗c5
16. c3   ♖a4

The newly-mobile rook is introduced with the threat 17...♖xd4.

17. ♗e2   ...

17. b4 won't do because of 17...
罝xb4. By moving the bishop from f1,
it alters the order in which Black captures on d4. Instead of delivering
mate, Black wins a pawn.

17. ...   ♗xd4+
18. cxd4   罝xd4

Another striking positional div-
idend paid by Black's tactics is that
18...罝xd4 holds the f4-pawn, so the c1-
bishop is still wrapped up.

19. b3   ...

Annotators have written that
White must have been pleased to make
a threat to skewer, but White was act-
ing more out of necessity — how else
to develop the bishop?

19. ...   ♘f6
20. ♗b2   罝d2
21. ♗h5+   ♘xh5!

Part of the game's charm lies in
this sacrificial move. White gets to
grab an inactive rook, while the black
knight is instrumental in the attack
against the white king.

22. ♗xh8   f3

Making way for the knight to en-
croach further, while threatening 23...
f2+ plus 24...♗f5 and 25...♗d3+.

23. gxf3   ♘f4

Jumping in with the idea to introduce crushing new force. Black
wants to play 24...♗h3, threatening
25...罝g2+ 26. ♔f1 罝f2+ 27. ♔e1 (27.
♔g1 ♘e2#) ♘d3+ 28. ♔d1 ♗g2 29 罝a2
♗xf3+ with the powerful minor piece
configuration from chapter 18, and
mate shortly.

24. ♗e5   ...

The earliest recorded example of
Capablanca's Mate would have been
24. 罝e1 罝g2+ 25. ♔f1 罝f2+ 26. ♔g1 ♗h3
(threatening 27...罝f1+ 28. 罝xf1 ♘e2#)
27. 罝xh3 ♘xh3+ 28. ♔h1 罝h2#.

24. ...   罝g2+
25. ♔f1   罝f2+
26. ♔e1   ♘d3+
0-1

27. ♔d1 g2 28. 罝g1 ♘xe5, and
White will lose a rook to the threatened ...♘xf3.

Game 22

Budapest 1928
White: J.R. Capablanca
Black: Kornel Havasi
Queen's Gambit Accepted

1. d4   d5
2. c4   e6

If Black wants to accept the gambit, he should play 2...dxc4.

3. ♘f3   dxc4
4. e4   c5
5. ♗xc4   cxd4
6. ♘xd4   ♘f6
7. ♘c3   ...

Compare this to a typical Queen's
Gambit Accepted — 1. d4 d5 2. c4 dxc4
3. ♘f3 ♘f6 4. e3 e6 5. ♗xc4 c5 6. ♘c3
cxd4 — White usually plays 7. exd4 to

move forward in the center while freeing the queen's bishop, at the cost of having an isolated pawn. In the position at hand, White has the better center plus the mobile pieces, but without the positional defect.

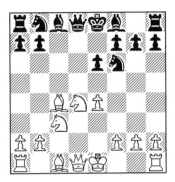

7. ...   a6

Dan Heisman's "A Guide to P-R3" at chesscafe.com suggests when not to play P-R3. 7...a6 is of so little use that it doesn't resemble any of the teacher's examples.

8. 0-0   ♗c5
9. ♗e3   ♘bd7

The position is the same as Capablanca-Bogoljubow, Moscow 1925, except that White is further ahead in development for the inclusion of 0-0 and ...a7-a6, which makes his sacrifice on e6 stronger. Forget that a master shouldn't be in Havasi's pickle at move 9; consider his not recalling Capablanca's win against Bogoljubow.

Today, gamescores are shared around the globe in real time — professional chessplayers are expected to be familiar with games from the last hour. Three decades ago, one was the best-informed chessplayer on his block if he invested in Russian chess

newspapers, and some were envied for assembling complete sets of the *Chess Informant*, a twice-yearly anthology of master games from around the world. These days you cannot give *Informants* away because the content has been digitized.

If you've never seen chess periodicals from 80 years ago, it's a culture shock to recognize how slowly news got around. Three years after the fact, it's possible Havasi had not even seen Capablanca-Bogoljubow.

10. ♗xe6!   ...

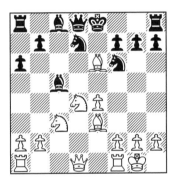

10. ...   fxe6
11. ♘xe6   ♕a5

Bogoljubow had ...♕b6 to fork, but here White's development tells on 11... ♕b6 12. ♘xc5 ♘xc5 13. ♘a4, when 13... ♕a5 isn't check.

12. ♘xg7+   ♔f7
13. ♘f5   ♘e5

Better is 13...♘b6 to block the b-file, so that Black can answer 14. ♕b3+ with 14...♗e6.

14. ♕b3+   ♔g6

Black's king is likely to perish after 14...♔e8 15. ♖ad1.

15. ♖ac1   ...

White threatens 16. ♗xc5 ♕xc5 17. ♘d5 with discovered attack, followed by 18. ♘f4+ and checkmate soon.

15. ...   ♗f8

Black ought to treat this position as if he is ahead in material — the three pawns White has for the piece are not yet menacing — and exchange one of the attackers by 15...♗xf5 or 15...♗xe3 (though 16. fxe3 introduces a rook).

16. ♘e2   ...

Threatens mate in four starting with 17. ♘f4+.

16. ...   h5

17. ♖fd1   ...

Developing the last unused piece (inactive force) with a threat. 18. ♘f4+ ♔h7 19. ♘d5 (idea: 20. ♖xc8 ♖xc8 21. ♕xb7+) ♘xd5 20. ♖xd5 is a winning fork because the newly developed rook stops 20...♕c7 to defend the e5-knight.

17. ...   ♖g8

18. ♘f4+   ♔h7

19. ♗b6   ...

A misstep. 19. ♘d5 is better.

19. ...   ♕b5

20. ♖c7+   ♔h8

21. ♕xb5   axb5

22. ♖d8   ♖xa2?

Losing. Chess Stars assessed 22...♗b4 23. ♖xg8+ ♔xg8 24. ♘h6+ ♔f8 25. f3 ♔e8 as unclear.

23. ♖dxc8   ♘c4

Black threatens mate on the back rank, and also attacks the bishop. He counted on this double threat when he played 22...♖xa2.

24. h3   ♘xb6

25. ♖xf8   ...

Threatening 26. ♘g6#, while 25...♖xf8 26. ♘g6+ ♔g8 27. ♖g7# is Capablanca's Mate.

25. ...   ♘fd7

26. ♖f7   ♖xb2

27. ♘d5   1-0

Game 23

São Paulo 1927
White: J.R. Capablanca
Black: A. Souza Campos
Owen's Defense

1. e4   b6

Rev. Owen's move isn't as sound as 1...g6. Both moves do the same for center control and development, but 1...g6 brings Black one move closer to castling.

2. d4   ♗b7

3. ♗d3   ...

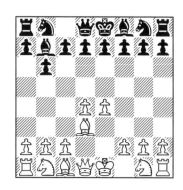

3. ... e6

The gambit 3...f5 4. exf5 ♗xg2 5. ♕h5+ g6 6. fxg6 ♗g7 (6...♘f6 7. gxh7+ ♘xh5 ♗g6#) has been put out of business by 7. ♕f5.

4. ♘f3 ...

Consider this most general formula for winning a chess game: obtain better center control, development, and king safety, and then from that superior position, attack the enemy king by opening files for the major.

Then take Morphy's invention 4. ♘h3. After two center pawn moves, White has a better center. The quickest kingside development — ♗d3, ♘h3, 0-0 — puts White ahead in development and king safety. Then White can push the f-pawn until the f1-rook is unleashed. You'd think that tidy scheme might have appealed to Capablanca.

4. ... c5
5. 0-0 ...

An alternative is 5. c3 d5 6. e5, which transposes to a French Defense that is less agreeable to Black, who should prefer to have his queen on b6 to help press on d4. 5. 0-0 makes a Sicilian Defense that favors White because Black's queenside motion ... a7-a6 plus ...b7-b5 lags. Capablanca's opinions were that the French is good and the Sicilian is porous, so it follows that he opted for the Sicilian transposition.

5. ... cxd4
6. ♘xd4 ...

The crux of the Sicilian is that White gives up center pawn for wing pawn but gains time with the recapture on d4, while Black — the pawn on

his fourth rank having disappeared — loses space. If Black tries for ...b6-b5 later, it will represent another loss of time as the pawn has already moved once.

6. ... ♘e7

Excusable if 7...♘bc6 is next. Otherwise 6...d6 plus 7...♘f6 to develop with a threat is better.

7. ♘c3 ...

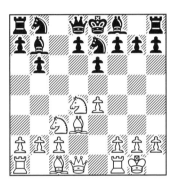

The holes in Black's position show on 7. ♘b5 a6 8. ♘d6#.

7. ... ♘g6

7...♘bc6 8. ♗e3 ♘xd4 9. ♗xd4 ♘c6 comes forward with a threat, and then 10. ♗e3 ♗c5 develops with another. 7...♘g6 doesn't use inactive force, and it creates a target for f4-f5 if White desires.

8. ♗e3 ♗c5
9. ♕h5 ...

White couldn't develop with a threat, but 9. ♕h5 develops with a threat to threaten—if the d4-knight moves, it discovers an attack on c5. For instance, 9...♘c6 would lose a pawn to 10. ♘xc6 and 11. ♗xc5.

9. ... 0-0
10. ♖ad1 ♗xd4

Peculiar, but it enables ...♘c6 without losing a pawn.

11. ♗xd4   ♘c6
12. ♗e3   e5

It seemed Black was heading for ... ♘ge5, but 12...e5 weakens the a2-g8 diagonal permanently, and the d-file further. 12...♖c8 uses inactive force, and makes c4 a more perilous square for the d3-bishop.

13. ♗c4   ♔h8

Black is running out of moves that keep him in the game, but 13...♔h8 enables White to come forward with threats, and leaves the rook tied to the f7-pawn. 13...♖c8 had to be more constructive.

14. ♖d6   ...

A pleasing move that fills the hole in Black's position, threatens 15. ♗xf7 ♖xf7 16. ♖xg6, and makes room for the last inactive piece.

14. ...   ♕e7
15. ♖fd1   ...

I ask myself: "If you write 'developing with a threat' whenever it applies, will it make a dull book, or make an essential point?"

15. ...   ♖ad8

16. ♗g5   f6

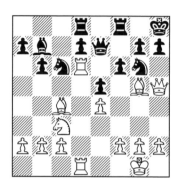

17. ♕xg6   ...

This game was first intended for the chapter on Greco's Mate.

17. ...   hxg6
18. ♖6d3   ♖f7

A much better defense was 18...d5 19. ♘xd5 ♖xd5 plus 20...♗c8.

19. ♘d5   ♕c5
20. ♖h3+   ♔g8
21. ♘xf6+   ♔f8

If 21...gxf6, then 22. ♗xf6 plus 23. ♖h8# is an example of Mate no. 9 (Chapter 14).

22. ♖h8+   ♔e7
23. ♖e8+!   ♖xe8
24. ♖xd7+   ♔f8
25. ♖xf7#   1-0

Chapter 7

Greco's Sacrifice

The Greco sacrifice is so rich and broad in scope that it occurs in games between both gradeschoolers and world champions (Anand-Karpov, Las Palmas 1996).

The Art of the Checkmate said: "A complete description ... would need at least 100 pages and cannot be included in this book, especially as [it] does not necessarily lead to a forced mate." Vuković devoted 25 pages to the Greco theme in *The Art of Attack in Chess*, and László Polgár gives many examples in *Chess: 5334 Problems, Combinations and Games*.

A bishop sacrifice pierces the king's fortress.

1. &xh7+   &xh7
2. ♘g5+   ...

Then the knight clears the d1-h5 diagonal for the queen. One prerequisite is that the knight land safely on g5.

2. ...   &g8

The defender's king usually has to flee his castle with 2...&h6 or 2...&g6. The attacker cannot always calculate all the way to mate, so he should be prepared to bring up reinforcements.

3. ♕h5   ...

A second requirement is that the defender be unable to guard the checkmating square. Look for a c8-bishop that can run to f5, or a d7-knight that can spring to f6 to stop ♕h7#.

Game 24

Stockholm 1912
White: Sundström
Black: Holm
Petroff's Defense

1. e4   e5
2. ♘f3   ♘f6
3. ♘xe5   d6
4. ♘f3   ...

4. ♘xf7 makes for the most interesting games.

4. ...   ♘xe4
5. ♘c3   ...

This method of meeting the Petroff grew in popularity when White players saw that it develops with a threat; their queenside is freed with the recapture; and whatever theory Black relies on following 5. d4 goes to waste.

5. ...   ♞xc3
6. dxc3   ♝e7
7. ♝d3

The Greco pattern is forming.

7. ...   0-0

The sacrifice at h7 doesn't work yet. If 8. ♝xh7+ ♚xh7 9. ♞g5+, the knight will be captured, so White supports the knight's leap.

8. h4   ♜e8

Inhibiting the h7-sacrifice again, because ...♝xg5+ will be a discovered check. White brings up new force to block the e-line, an example of how recognizing checkmating patterns aids in planning.

9. ♝e3   ♞c6?

White twice introduced new force as part of a plan to make the Greco sacrifice. With 9...♞c6, Black reveals that he played 8...♜e8 unwittingly. Learning checkmating patterns helps one create wins and avoid losses.

10. ♝xh7+   ♚xh7
11. ♞g5+   ♚g6

8. h4 supported the knight's jump and dissuaded Black from capturing because 11...♝xg5 12. hxg5+ introduces an entire rook.

12. h5+   ♚f6
13. ♛f3+   ♚f5

13...♚e5 14. ♛e4+ ♚f6 15. ♞h7# is a pretty queen-and-knight coordination.

14. g4   ...

Bringing up more new force with the threat of 15. ♛xf5#.

14. ...   ♛d7
15. ♞e4+   ♚e5
16. ♛f4+   ♚d5
17. 0-0-0+   ♚c4
18. ♞xd6#   1-0

Game 25

Buenos Aires 1911
White: J.R. Capablanca
Black: L. Molina Carranza
Queen's Gambit Declined

1. d4   d5
2. c4   e6
3. ♞c3   ♞f6
4. ♝g5   ♞bd7
5. e3   c6
6. ♞f3   ♝e7

7. cxd5   ...

White usually prefers to give Black the option of playing ...dxc4 as long as possible. 7. ♗d3 is playable, but then 7...dxc4 8. ♗xc4 uses two tempi to accomplish what could have been done in one. Therefore, 7. ♖c1 and 7. ♕c2 are seen most often as White tries to win the tempo battle. With 7. cxd5 exd5, White looks ahead to a middle-game where his b-pawn pushes to b5, resulting in a weakening of Black's queenside pawns. Some players seem to be versed in nothing but this "minority attack" — they are some of the dreariest opponents one can face, which often helps them.

7. ...   ♘xd5

A bad move, failing to maintain a pawn in the center. 7...exd5 also frees the c8-bishop (the minority attackers think the bad bishop has little future anyway).

8. ♗xe7   ♘xe7

Another bad move. 7. ♗xe7 enabled Black to develop a piece with 7...♕xe7.

9. ♗d3   ...

Even though Black has made two poor positional moves, he is far from dead, because he has so far avoided tactical error. Players who think they can improve their opening play by memorizing book moves should learn that the costliest opening miscues are tactical, and they can improve their opening play by studying tactics. Black is still in the game, so White has to keep playing well. He brings up a new piece to control the center while preparing castling.

9. ...   c5

Yet another weak move. The opening of the position favors the side that's ahead in development. 9...0-0 doesn't

plow into the Greco sacrifice because the d7-knight can get to f6 to ward off checkmate at h7.

10. 0-0   0-0?

A tactical mistake, so it is the worst of the four. Black can't recapture on c5 because the knight defends against the Greco pattern.

11. dxc5!   ♘xc5
12. ♗xh7+   ♔xh7
13. ♘g5+   ...

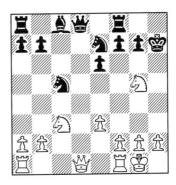

13. ...   ♔g6

White is winning after 13...♔g8 14. ♕h5 ♖e8 15. ♖ad1 ♗d7 (the queen must keep in touch with the e8-rook, else ♕xf7+) 16. ♕xf7+ ♔h8 17. b4 with ♘ce4 to come.

14. ♕g4   f5
15. ♕g3   ♔h6
16. ♕h4+   ♔g6
17. ♕h7+   ...

Even if White cannot completely calculate the effects of 17. ♕h7+, he must believe that if he keeps bringing new pieces to the attack that he will succeed. 17. ♕g3 ♔h6 18. ♕h4+ ♔g6 19. ♕g3 making a draw is no way to play chess.

17. ...   ♔f6

If 17...♚xg5, then 18. ♕xg7+ ♚h5 19. f4 with 20. ♖f3 wins.

18. e4   ...

Bringing up another unit with the threat to expose the king further by 19. e5+ ♚xe5 20. ♕xg7+. If Black captures on e4, then White's queen's knight joins the attack.

18. ...   ♘g6
19. exf5   exf5
20. ♖ad1   ...

The biggest unused piece comes in with the biggest threat. If Black moves his queen to e7, c7, or b6, she will be forked, while 20...♕a5 meets the pawn fork 21. b4, and 20...♕e8 invites the f1-rook into play.

20. ...   ♘d3
21. ♕h3   ...

There is still no clear win in sight, so White carries on with a doubly threatening move (22. ♘h7+ is in the mix), and if the d3-knight can be budged, then White can deploy his inactive rook.

21. ...   ♘df4

21...♘gf4 keeps the queen shielded, and if Black attempts the trick ...♕c7xc3, a knight on d3 also prevents ♕xc3 from coming with check.

22. ♕g3   ...

22. ...   ♕c7

White must remain vigilant. Black envisions tricks with ...♕xc3 plus ...♘e2+.

23. ♖fe1   ...

Bringing up more new force usually works better than grabbing stuff, like 23. ♘h7+ ♚f7 24. ♘xf8 ♕xc3.

23. ...   ♘e2+

23...♖h8 was better, keeping Black off a fork while mobilizing his rook. Black was desperate to get the queens off the board while his king was unsheltered.

24. ♖xe2   ♕xg3
25. ♘h7+   ...

This in-between move is necessary to save the knight. 25. ♘h7+ was played between capture and recapture on g3.

25. ...   ♚f7
26. hxg3   ♖h8

Black played the whole game poorly. 26...♖e8 makes it harder for White to coordinate against e6.

27. ♘g5+   ♚f6
28. f4

Brings up more new force with the killer threat 29. ♖d6+.

1-0

Game 26

Barcelona 1935
Simultaneous exhibition
White: J.R. Capablanca
Black: A. Ribera Arnal
Caro-Kann Defense

1. e4 ...

The occasion was a 10-board simultaneous exhibition with clocks. Those are more difficult for the exhibitor, whose pause for thought at one board occurs while clocks are ticking at all the others.

1.	...	c6
2.	♘c3	d5
3.	♘f3	...

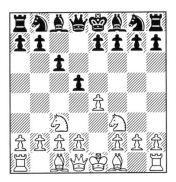

Smyslov played this Two Knights' variation of the Caro-Kann three times in the 1958 world championship match against Botvinnik. Fischer was very fond of it.

3. ... dxe4

Another way is 3...♗g4 4. h3 ♗xf3 5. ♕xf3 e6, where Black in a less roomy position exchanges his bad bishop right away.

4. ♘xe4 ♘d7

The value of White's most rapid development shows if Black plays in typical Caro-Kann fashion: 4...♗f5 5. ♘g3 ♗g6 6. h4 h6 7. ♘e5 ♗h7 8. ♕h5 g6 9. ♗c4 e6 10. ♕e2, and Black's position is horrible.

5. d4 ♘gf6

The game transposes to a standard Caro-Kann. The most popular move is 6. ♘xf6+, and then after 6...♘xf6, White's control of e5 is more secure. That, however, doesn't agree with the general principle of avoiding exchanges that free an opponent's cramped position.

| 6. | ♘g3 | e6 |
| 7. | ♗d3 | ♗e7 |

Black's road to equality is a little easier with 7...c5, removing or isolating the white d-pawn.

| 8. | 0-0 | 0-0 |
| 9. | ♕e2 | c5 |

9...c5 came a bit late, because White can play a menacing rook to the d-file.

| 10. | ♖d1 | ♕c7 |
| 11. | ♗g5 | b6 |

The f6-knight and the e6-pawn are both pinned because the e7-bishop is hanging. 11...♖e8 to guard the bishop is one possibility, after which ... ♘f8 to free the c8-bishop is perhaps in store. Also, 11...h6 would be a relief. Chessplayers frequently play P-KR3 — weakening their king's position — because they can't think of anything useful to do, but here White can't maintain the pin on the f6-knight because 12. ♗h4 g5 traps the bishop.

12. d5! ...

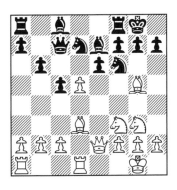

White's threat to win a pawn on e6 forces Black to open lines.

12. ...   ♘xd5

Black's attempt to trap the queen fails: 12...exd5 13. ♕xe7 ♖e8 14. ♗xh7+ ♔xh7 15. ♕xf7. If Black tries to keep the lines closed with 12...♕d6, his queen is threatened with a discovery after 13. ♗c4, and then a fork: 13...exd5 14. ♘f5.

13. ♗xe7   ♘xe7
14. ♗xh7+   ♔xh7
15. ♘g5+   ...

A pitfall for the greedy: 15. ♕e4+ ♔g8 16. ♕xa8 ♗b7 17. ♕xa7 ♖a8.

15. ...   ♔g8
16. ♖xd7!   ...

So 17. ♕h5 cannot be met by 17...♘f6.

16. ...   ♕xd7

16...♗d7 is better, but Black envisions a "cheapo" on the back rank.

17. ♕h5   ♖d8
18. ♕xf7+   ♔h8

White must beware of 19. ♘h5 ♕d1+.

19. h4   ♘f5
20. ♘h5   ...

Capablanca missed the best shot here: 20. ♕g6 ♔g8 21. ♘xf5 exf5 22. ♖e1, winning.

20. ...   ♕e8

Then Black didn't see his chance: 20...♕xf7 21. ♘xf7+ ♔g8 22. ♘xd8 ♗d7 23. ♘b7 ♗c6, and the knight is trapped.

21. ♘f6!   ♕f8

If 21...gxf6, then 22. ♕h7#.

22. ♕g6   ♕g8
23. ♕h7+!   ♕xh7
24. ♘f7#
1-0

Game 27

Providence 1922
White: J.R. Capablanca
Black: Hoffman
French Defense

1.   d4   e6

When Black answers 1. d4 with 1...e6 or 1...c6, Black is daring — maybe welcoming is a better word — White to transpose to a French or Caro-Kann by 2. e4, and White frequently does. It says something about the strength of 1. e4 that while 1...e6 and 1...c6 are considered reasonable defenses to 1. e4, they are thought not as strong against 1. d4 because the transpositions are enabled.

2.   e4   d5
3.   ♘c3   ♗b4

Winawer's 3...♗b4 is sharper than the Classical 3...♘f6 because it's more likely to provoke a quick ♕d1-g4 from White. On 3...♘f6, not only does White have to play e4-e5 to kick the knight away from covering g4, the f8-bishop still has to move for g7 to be exposed.

4.   ♗d3

The usual move is 4. e5, while 4. exd5 can be an improved Exchange French because the bishop is not as well placed for Black on b4 as it is on d6. 4. a3 ♗xc3+ 5. bxc3 dxe4 is a gambit worth exploring, as is 4. ♘e2 dxe4 5. a3.

Nothing is wrong with 4. ♗d3, but your neighborhood openings expert will dismiss it because it's easier for

Black to equalize in theory. What happens in practice is quite different from theory.

4.	...	♘c6
5.	♘f3	dxe4
6.	♗xe4	...

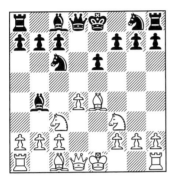

| 6. | ... | ♘ge7 |

Not as good as 6...♘f6, developing with a threat. If Black is worried about ♗xc6+, then 6...♗d7, and eventually Black can play ...♗c6 to get the bishop outside the e6-pawn. Some French defenders make that maneuver the basis for their opening play: 1. e4 e6 2. d4 d5 3. ♘c3 dxe4 4. ♘xe4 ♗d7 with ...♗c6 to follow.

7.	0-0	♗xc3
8.	bxc3	0-0
9.	♗xh7+	♔h8?

9...♔xh7 10. ♘g5+ ♔g6 11. ♕g4 f5 12. ♕g3 is unclear.

When chess educators discuss the Greco sacrifice, K-R1 is almost never mentioned as a reply to BxP+ because it is like giving up. If Black doesn't take the bishop, White gains a pawn for nothing while fatally weakening the black king position and preserving the attacking bishop.

Euwe talks about K-R1 in *Chess Master vs. Chess Amateur* because half of the moves in the book are amateur-class moves, and the other half are master-class moves designed to take advantage. Too many chess books are about how masters beat other masters, while too few are about how to beat patzers.

10.	♗d3	f6
11.	♘e5	...

Better than 11. ♘g5, when Black can cling to 11...g6.

| 11. | ... | fxe5 |

Black is entombed by 11...♕e8 12. ♘g6+ ♘xg6 13. ♕h5+ ♔g8 14. ♗xg6 ♖f7 15. ♕h7+ ♔f8 16. ♗a3+ ♘e7 17. ♕h8#.

12.	♕h5+	♔g8
13.	♗h7+	1-0

13...♔h8 14. ♗g6+ ♔g8 15. ♕h7# is another pattern one must know (in *The Art of the Checkmate*, it's Damiano's Bishop, or checkmate no. 12B).

Part II

Play Like Capablanca
(or at least passably well)

You must see all real threats, and that means you must also see the unreality of unreal threats.
— C.J.S. Purdy

Chapter 8

Bookstore Marketing and Other Tall Tales

A First Book of Morphy was my first book, using Morphy games to illustrate chess principles set down by grandmaster Fine in *Chess the Easy Way*. At times I feel like I did a disservice to some readers, who presumed that reciting Fine's dogma would make them chessplayers.

The unequaled chess teacher Cecil Purdy had this to say about general principles:

Chessplayers may be divided into three classes: those who don't know the principles, and are therefore very weak; those who know the principles and are less weak; and those who know how weak the principles are, and are strong.

Chessplayers are good when they're good at tactics and checkmates, consistently using inactive force and examining every threatening move, while recognizing — and ignoring — unreal threats.

Threats trump positional moves, and tactics trump principles (but threats and tactics should be based on positional goals grounded in principle!).

Play Like Capablanca!

Chess literature makes promises worthy of a late night infomercial: *How to Beat Anyone at Chess* (by someone named Kretschmer, who evidently can beat anyone at chess); *Perfect Your Chess*; *How to Crush Your Chess Opponents*.

On a tight schedule? Achieve chess excellence with a timetable: *Mensa Guide to Chess: 30 Days to Great Chess*; *Mastering Chess: A Course in 21 Lessons*; *From Beginner to Expert in 40 Lessons*.

Those are all real titles, which I thought I might mock by naming this book *Play Like Capablanca*, while making a pledge in the subtitle which is actually within reach: or passably well.

Play Chess Passably Well!

Your idea of playing chess passably well and Purdy's idea might be far apart (by Purdy's definition, "passably well" is enough to win the chess club championship in your town). Purdy said:

It is impossible to play chess even passably well unless you see all captures and checks at your own and your opponent's disposal, but seeing captures and checks is not enough. You must see all real threats, and that means you must also see the unreality of unreal threats.

In the cowboy movies of old, you knew who the bad guy was. He waved a six-shooter menacingly, while telling the comic relief sidekick to dance. Bad Guy would fire a couple of shots at Comic Relief's feet, and Comic Relief — fearing for his toes — would hop around.

Then the marshal enters the picture. When Bad Guy fires at Marshal's feet, he stands his ground, and for not dancing to the bad guy's tune, he can draw his own revolver and save the day.

The move is the most precious commodity in chess. While pieces and squares and units of time can be bartered, the rules say each side gets one move per turn. The player who makes the best use of his moves wins, usually by a gradual aggregation of positive moves. When a player makes an unreal threat — a move that looks menacing but can be ignored — it's a lost move, a negative entry on the ledger.

Students should get into the habits of making threatening moves whenever they can, and ignoring enemy threats whenever possible. Thousands of little kids are taught early to do the wrong thing: to defend a pawn instead of to ignore a threat.

White: Felix
Black: Sylvester

| 1. | e4 | e5 |
| 2. | ♕h5 | ... |

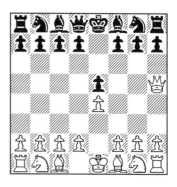

Other than 2. ♘f3, 2. ♕h5 — which Hikaru Nakamura actually played in a grandmaster tournament — is the only developing move that makes a threat, to which Black mustn't answer 2...♔e7?.

2. ...   ♘f6

Kids are instructed by poor chess teachers and other kids to dance for the six-shooter, but the hoppity 2... ♘c6 3. ♗c4 ♕e7 (or 3...♕f6) leads to stuffed, unwieldy games for Black.

The gambit 2...♘f6 can be recommended because while players are learning, they should cultivate the habit of making threatening moves. Also, 2...♘f6 ignores White's threat. The best thing to do about an opponent's threat is... nothing, if possible.

3. ♕xe5+ ...

2...♘f6 made White dance!

| 3. | ... | ♗e7 |
| 4. | ♘c3 | 0-0 |

The white royals stacked on the e-file, Black hastens to play ...♖e8.

| 5. | ♗c4 | ♖e8 |
| 6. | ♕g3 | ♘xe4 |

The old fork trick serves to gain a pawn majority in the center, while opening the e-file for the black rook.

7.	♘xe4	d5
8.	♗b3	♗d6

Not 8...dxe4, which does not threaten, and even blocks the road to the white king. This in-between move threatens, while enabling Black to capture on e4 with check.

9.	♕f3	♖xe4+
10.	♘e2	♗g4
0-1		

Chessplayers should never be scared of an opponent. Not their dads, not Capablanca, not even Kenny Fong, my childhood nemesis.

Strong players benefit from their reputations — their opponents frighten themselves into timid play, but if they used inactive force and examined all the threatening moves, then the better player has to prove himself by playing good moves more consistently.

Game 28

Washington 1909
White: J.R. Capablanca
Black: E. Adams
Three Knights' Game

1.	e4	e5
2.	♘f3	♘c6
3.	♘c3	...

This move cannot be recommended to inexpert players. It doesn't threaten, while the c3-square is better left to a pawn. For instance: 3. d4 (threatens to capture the e5-pawn) 3...exd4 4. c3 (threatens to win the center by taking on d4) 4...dxc3 5. ♘xc3, and White has achieved the same knight placement, but with more queenside mobility, while Black is absent from the center.

Or 3. ♗c4 ♗c5 4. b4! ♗xb4 5. c3 plus d2-d4 with a promising position.

In the 1980s, the Four Knights' Game was fashionable with grandmasters who used 3. ♘c3 to defer the Ruy López bishop development ♗f1-b5. Capablanca played the Three and Four Knights' Games as simple methods for enabling his opponents to make mistakes.

3.	...	♗c5

Chessplayers err early and often in the tamest positions, but their opponents must be tactically alert and capable.

4.	♘xe5	♘xe5

Black could compound the error with 4...♗xf2+ 5. ♔xf2 ♘xe5 6. d4, when White has an ideal center.

5.	d4	♗xd4

Another slip, forcing White to skewer with his queen. 5...♗d6 6. dxe5 ♗xe5 preserves the bishop, while Black has a minor menace of his own: to take on c3.

6.	♕xd4	♕f6

Breaking the skewer, and threatening to win the queen by the discovered attack 7...♘f3+.

7.	♘b5	...

The best defense is a counterattack. 7. ♗e3 guards the queen but does not threaten.

7. ...   ♔d8?

When the enemy moves, the first question to ask oneself is, "What are the threats?" After identifying the most serious threat, then one asks, "What if I pass? What if I let my opponent move again, and let him carry out that threat?"

Black needs to see that if he passes at move 7, allowing White to play 8. ♘xc7+, then 8...♔d8 threatens 9...♔xc7, while 9...♘f3+ is back in the picture. Then White could play 9. ♕c5, when 9...♖b8 is not so horrible for Black. Therefore, 8. ♘xc7+ is a threat that can be ignored.

If Black plays the attacking move 7...c6, then White has to change course and play 8. ♘d6+, which is also favorable, but a little less so.

8. ♕c5   ♘c6

Black overlooked the most serious threat, but he's in a hole anyway. For instance: 8...♘e7 9. ♕xc7+ ♔e8 10. ♘d6+ wins the queen, or 8...♘h6 9. ♕xc7+ ♔e8 10. h4 prepares to introduce the bishop.

9. ♕f8#   1-0

Game 29

Karlsbad 1929
White: J.R. Capablanca
Black: A. Becker
Queen's Gambit Declined

1. d4   ...

Chess authors are often prejudiced against informal games, games played at odds, and short games, but Golombek thought this miniature worthy of inclusion in *Capablanca's Hundred Best Games*. He was impressed with the tactics at the end, arising after the opening in which Capablanca ignored a threat to his structure.

1. ...   d5
2. c4   e6
3. ♘f3   ♘d7

3...♘d7 usually transposes to a typical Queen's Gambit Declined, with little independent significance unless Black opts for a fast ...♗f8-b4 plus ...c7-c5.

4. ♘c3   ♘gf6
5. ♗f4   dxc4

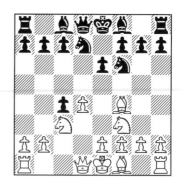

Eighty years later, theory still recommends ...dxc4 plus ...♘d5 as a good way to meet ♗f4 in the Queen's Gambit, but Black gets better results from 5...♗b4, developing.

6. e3   ♘d5
7. ♗xc4   ...

For ignoring the positional threat ...♘xf4, White gains an additional developing move and a bit more space. London System (1. d4 2. ♘f3 3. ♗f4) practitioners get the same kind of option — for instance, 1. ♘f3 d5 2. d4 c6 3. c3 ♗f5 4. ♗f4 ♘d7 5. e3 ♕b6 6. b3 ♘gf6 7. ♗d3 g6 8. ♕c2 e6 9. ♘bd2 ♘h5 10. 0-0 ♘xf4 11. exf4, Chapman-Kasparov, London 2001.

The same idea applies in king pawn openings: Steil-I.Agrest, Women's Olympiad, Dresden 2008: 1. e4 e5 2. ♗c4 ♘c6 3. d3 d6 4. ♘f3 ♘a5 5. 0-0 ♘xc4 6. dxc4 ♘f6 7. ♖e1 ♗e7 8. ♕d3 0-0 9. ♘c3 c6 10. b3, where White's pawn structure complements the remaining bishop, and she has a grip on d5.

The whole idea seems to lose merit if the player loses control of the center. For instance, Rubinstein-Capablanca, London 1922: 1. d4 ♘f6 2. ♘f3 d5 3. ♗f4 e6 4. e3 ♗d6 5. ♘bd2 ♗xf4 6. exf4 c5 — and then White voluntarily gave up the center, after which the game was soon drawn — 7. dxc5 ♕c7 8. g3 ♕xc5 9. ♗d3 ♘c6 10. c3 0-0 11. 0-0 b5 12. ♘e5 ♗b7 13. ♕e2 ½-½.

7.	...	♘xf4
8.	exf4	♗d6
9.	g3	♘f6
10.	0-0	0-0
11.	♕e2	...

White's development is characteristic of typical isolated d-pawn positions. Compare this position to a Caro-Kann Panov Attack in which Black wastes a few moves: 1. e4 c6 2. c4 d5 3. cxd5 cxd5 4. exd5 ♘f6 5. d4 ♘bd7 6. ♘c3 ♘b6 7. ♗g5 ♘bxd5 8. ♗xf6 ♘xf6 9. ♗c4 e6 10. f4 ♗e7 11. ♘f3 0-0 12. 0-0 ♗d6 13. g3 ♔h8 14. ♕e2.

11.	...	b6

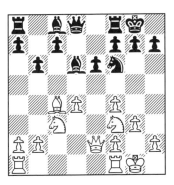

12. ♖fd1   ...

A little offbeat, since the king's rook should prefer the open e-file, but Black's c-pawn is usually on c6. In this position, Black might be more inclined toward ...c5, so White dissuades Black's center action: 12...c5 13. dxc5 bxc5 14. ♘b5 ♘e8 15. ♕d3 wins a piece.

12.	...	♗b7
13.	♖ac1	a6

Black found it difficult to choose a move in his cramped position, but ... a7-a6 is pointless, because White will not waste time on ♘b5xd6. Meanwhile, Black has immobilized his queen's rook and bishop by tying them to the defense of a6. Better was the development 13...♕e7 with a view toward ...♖fd8 and ...c5.

14.	♗d3	...

The bishop bites on granite at e6, but from d3 it has clear sight of the black king.

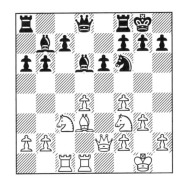

14.	...	♗b4

Botvinnik followed Capablanca as world champion partly because he studied Capablanca. This position arose in Botvinnik-Ragozin, Leningrad Championship 1930, where

Black played the better move 14...♕e7, but White won with 15. ♘e4 ♖fd8 16. ♘xf6+ ♕xf6 17. ♗e4 ♗xe4 18. ♕xe4 c5 19. ♘e5 cxd4 20. ♖xd4 ♗c5 21. ♖d7 ♕f5 22. ♕b7 ♖ab8 23. ♕f3 f6 24. g4 1-0.

15. ♘e4   ...

Threatening 16. ♘xf6+, when Black must either ruin his castled position or drop a pawn. 15...♘d5 meets the threat while putting another guard on c7.

15. ...   ♕d5?

A mistake. Black is hoping for 16. ♘xf6+ gxf6, when Black's threats along the h1-a8 diagonal compel White to settle for a draw: 17. ♖xc7 ♕xf3 18. ♖xb7 ♕xb7 19. ♕g4+ ♔h8 20. ♕h4 f5 21. ♕f6+ ♔g8 22. ♕g5+.

16. ♘fg5!   ...

A powerful double threat. The first menace is 17. ♘xf6+ gxf6 18. ♗xh7+ ♔h8 19. ♗e4.

16. ...   ♘e8

If 16...♘d7, then 17. ♖xc7 threatens 18. ♖xd7 ♕xd7 19. ♘f6+ with a winning attack.

17. ♘xh7   ...

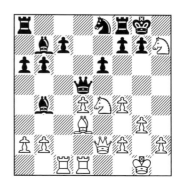

17. ...   f5

17...♔xh7 loses the queen to 18. ♘f6+. Best is 17...♗e7, ready to capture a knight on g5, even though White can take on f8.

18. ♘hg5!   1-0

White's threats of 19. ♕h5 and 19. ♗c4 are crushing.

Chapter 9

The Back-Rank Mate

Many of the puzzles in Gillam's *Simple Checkmates*, and most in *Bobby Fischer Teaches Chess*, pertain to the back rank, which is valuable because those mates are likelier to arise than others. As soon as someone castles, the stage is set.

Some back-rank combinations are most lovely in their logic.

Vrnjačka Banja 1966
White: D. Minić
Black: K. Honfi

23. ?

The same theme is explored at fantastic length in E.Z. Adams-C. Torre, New Orleans 1920, which is one of the most brilliant games ever — if it truly happened. The reader is encouraged to look it up — the back-rank combination is extraordinary.

Two of Capablanca's most famous games feature back-rank checkmating ideas.

Game 30

New York 1918
White: J.R. Capablanca
Black: Marc Fonaroff
Ruy López

1. e4   ...

It's the conclusion of this game that represents Capablanca most often in combination anthologies , while the game as a whole is Capablanca's best-known miniature. Players form an impression of Capablanca that many of his games must be this spectacular — the same is true of Morphy and his brilliancies — but it isn't so. Both cultivated their gems in proper positional play: achieving better center control, development, and king safety while using inactive force and examining threats.

1. ...   e5
2. ♘f3   ♘c6
3. ♗b5   ♘f6

Capablanca reached this position 25 times, and though he excelled in the Four Knights' Game, only twice did he transpose with 4. ♘c3. If he was in the mood for the Four Knights, he would play 3. ♘c3 instead of 3. ♗b5.

4. 0-0   d6

Solid, but during the 2000 world championship match, Kramnik's 4...♘xe4 5. d4 ♘d6 6. ♗xc6 dxc6 7. dxe5 ♘f5 was an impossible nut to crack.

5. d4   ♗d7
6. ♘c3   ♗e7

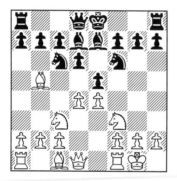

Capablanca reached this position from a Four Knights move order a few times, most notably in Game 3 of the 1921 world championship match with Lasker.

7. ♖e1   exd4

It's vital for López players of either color to understand why Black has to give up the center (it's startling to see how many do not). On 7...0-0, Black loses at least a pawn to 8. ♗xc6 ♗xc6 9. dxe5 dxe5 10. ♕xd8 ♖axd8 11. ♘xe5 ♗e4 (11...♗d7 limits the damage to a single pawn, but 11...♘xe4 loses a piece to 12. ♘xc6) 12. ♘xe4 ♘xe4 13. ♘d3 (pinning, while preventing a catastrophe like 13. ♖xe4 ♖d1+) 13...f5 14. f3 ♗c5+ 15. ♘xc5 ♘xc5 16. ♗g5 (developing with one threat to capture and another threat to fork) ♖d5 17. ♗e7 ♖e8 18. c4 (driving off the guard) 1-0, named the "Dresden Trap" after Tarrasch-Marco, Dresden 1892.

8. ♘xd4   ♘xd4

Black is trying to relieve his cramped position with exchanges, but each of his trades brings a white piece forward. In Game 12 of the 1921 world championship match, Capablanca castled as Black, and then Lasker played 9. ♗f1 to avoid exchanges.

9. ♕xd4   ♗xb5
10. ♘xb5   0-0
11. ♕c3   ...

Making room for the knight to centralize while threatening c7. It is absolutely essential — this can't be stressed strongly enough — that before White plays 11. ♕c3, he thinks "What if Black does nothing? What if Black passes on his move?" In other words, can Black ignore the threat?

What if White is allowed to carry out his threat? 12. ♘xc7 ♖c8 pins the knight. What about 12. ♕xc7 ♕xc7 13. ♘xc7 ♖c8, skewering, followed by ...♖xc2 with a very active rook? If that were true, then Black should nonchalantly go about developing with 11...♖e8. But after 12. ♕xc7 ♕xc7 13. ♘xc7 ♖c8, White has an additional threatening move — 14. ♘d5 — which affords him the time to shore up the c2-pawn, so therefore 12. ♕xc7 is a real threat, one that cannot be ignored.

In order to play this game passably well, one must get into the habit of examining every threatening move, while recognizing the unreality of unreal threats.

11. ...   c6

The best defense is a counterattack, and Black can develop with a threat: 11...♕d7, when White can be greedy and fall behind in development with 12. ♕xc7 ♕xb5 13. ♕xe7 ♖fe8 14. ♕xd6 ♘xe4. 11...♕d7 beats 11...c6 because active piece moves almost always beat a pawn move, while the pawn move itself makes d6 backward, and there the game turns.

12. ♘d4   ♘d7

Black shuffles his minor pieces to get his bishop outside the d6-pawn, and to centralize his knight.

13. ♘f5   ♗f6
14. ♕g3   ♘e5
15. ♗f4   ♕c7
16. ♖ad1   ...

Three moves in row — two developing moves — take aim at d6.

16. ...   ♖ad8

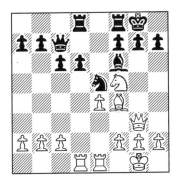

17. ♖xd6!

Black's position collapses. White threatens 18. ♖xf6 or 18. ♗xe5, for starters.

17. ...   ♖xd6
18. ♗xe5   ...

18...♗xe5 here will lose a rook to the double threat 19. ♕xe5, but Black thinks he found a shocker!

18. ...   ♖d1

The mate threat also discovers the queen's attack on e5.

19. ♖xd1   ♗xe5

Black's swift coordination of queen and bishop skewers white queen and h2-pawn, while the b2-pawn is attacked directly. Did 18...♖d1 save the day for Black?!

20. ♘h6+   ♔h8
21. ♕xe5!   ♕xe5
22. ♘xf7+   1-0

In retrospect, 18...♕a5 was necessary, but thank goodness Fonaroff found his tricky 18...♖d1, else this game wouldn't have achieved immortal status.

Game 31

Moscow 1914
White: Ossip Bernstein
Black: J.R. Capablanca
Queen's Gambit Declined

1. d4   d5
2. c4   ...

Since the Göttingen manuscript, circa 1490, the Queen's Gambit has been known as a fine opening for White. With 1...d5, Black interferes with White's ideal start of 1. d4 2. e4, so logic suggests that White deflect or capture the d5-pawn following 2. c4.

2. ... e6

2...e6 and 2...c6 are the most solid replies. Other moves are confrontational (2...e5, 2...c5) or active (2...♘c6, 2...♘f6, 2...♗f5), but Black is less able to maintain a pawn in the center.

3. ♘c3 ♘f6

Now that Black has supported his d5-pawn, he might play 3...c5 in an improved move order. Capablanca used the Tarrasch Defense in his most remarkable 23rd match game against Marshall.

4. ♘f3 ♗e7

Black is playing sensibly — his center pawn is maintained, and he's going to castle next. In the modern fashion, Black might delay the king's bishop development indefinitely: 4...c6 (most popular, but the c8-bishop is further stifled, so Black goes about freeing it) 5. e3 ♘bd7 6. ♗d3 dxc4 7. ♗xc4 b5 8. ♗d3 ♗b7 9. 0-0 a6 (guarding the b5-pawn before moving the c-pawn) 10. e4 c5 11. d5 ♕c7 12. dxe6 fxe6 13. ♗c2 c4 14. ♕e2 ♗d6 was the course of dozens of 21st-century master games, quite the opposite of Capablanca's play in 1914.

5. ♗g5 0-0
6. e3 ♘bd7
7. ♖c1 ...

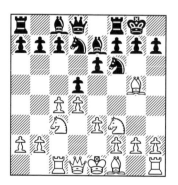

7. ... b6

7...b6 has some flaws, both of which are exposed by White's reply. First, a bishop on b7 might forever be blocked by the d5-pawn. Second, the c7-pawn is made backward. Capablanca developed a much better defensive scheme: 7...c6 keeps the c-file blocked, then 8. ♗d3 dxc4 9. ♗xc4 ♘d5, and after Black's cramped position is relieved by minor-piece exchanges, he can spring the queen's bishop: 10. ♗xe7 ♕xe7 11. 0-0 ♘xc3 12. ♖xc3 e5.

8. cxd5 ...

The c1-rook bears on the c7-pawn, which can no longer help itself by pushing to c6 because its supporting b-pawn also moved.

8. ... exd5
9. ♕a4 ...

By probing the light squares on the queenside, White brings about some exchanges, which favors the side playing against weak pawn(s).

9. ... ♗b7

Golombek recommended that Black sacrifice a pawn with 9...c5 10. ♕c6 ♖b8 11. ♘xd5 ♘xd5 12. ♕xd5 ♗b7 13. ♗xe7 ♕xe7, with better development.

10. ♗a6 ♗xa6
11. ♕xa6 c5
12. ♗xf6 ♘xf6
13. dxc5 bxc5

For lack of a better term, these are called "hanging pawns." The c- and d-pawns are not exactly isolated because they have each other as a neighbor, and neither is technically backward until its neighbor advances. Hanging pawns have the potential to become very weak, but also very strong.

14. 0-0   ♛b6

Developing with a threat and a gain of time because the white queen must retreat. 15. ♕xb6 would be a mistake, as 15...axb6 strengthens the black pawns and mobilizes the a8-rook for free.

15. ♕e2   c4

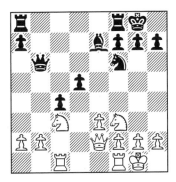

Even though the d5-pawn is made backward and d4 becomes a dream square for a knight, Black's bishop is freer, and the b2-pawn becomes a target under restraint.

16. ♖fd1   ♖fd8
17. ♘d4   ♝b4
18. b3?   ...

A critical error, because whether pawns are exchanged on c4 or Black advances to c3, the result is a passed pawn for Black. Black was perhaps considering 18...♖ab8 plus 19...♝xc3 20. bxc3 ♘e4, when it is White's pawns that are weak, and the knight looks forward to ...♘c5-d3. For White to hold the balance, 18. ♕c2 makes room for the knight, then 18...♖ab8 19. ♘ce2 sidesteps ...♝xc3 while the white knights are entrenched.

18. ...   ♖ac8

The simplest developing move for the only inactive piece, but it's part of the Capablanca mystique that his pieces somehow found the best squares most naturally. Rooks belong behind passed pawns.

19. bxc4   dxc4
20. ♖c2   ...

A purposeless move. Rooks belong behind passed pawns because when the passed pawn advances, a rook behind it gains mobility, but a rook in front of an advancing pawn loses mobility. The c1-rook could get out from in front of the pawn with 20. ♖b1, while 20. h3 might be what Bernstein would have chosen in hindsight.

20. ...   ♝xc3
21. ♖xc3   ♘d5

Black's plan is to attack the blockader, and then push the passed pawn.

22. ♖c2

22. ♖xc4 ♘c3 demonstrates the X-ray ability of the c8-rook, and wins rook for knight.

22. ...   c3
23. ♖dc1   ♖c5

No matter how many times I see this game, the repetition that follows 23...♖c5 reminds me of the "Duck season!" "Rabbit season!" dialogue from the Bugs Bunny/Daffy Duck cartoons directed by Chuck Jones.

24. ♘b3   ...

"It's rabbit season!"

24. ...   ♖c6

"Duck season!"

25. ♘d4

"Rabbit season!!"

25. ...	**♖c7**
26. ♘b5	**♖c5**
27. ♘xc3?	**...**

"It's duck season! Fire!" Had Capablanca played 23...♖c7, Bernstein might've given this a little more thought.

27. ...	**♘xc3**
28. ♖xc3	**♖xc3**
29. ♖xc3	**♕b2!**
0-1	

Chapter 10

Greco's Mate

Gioachino Greco had a cool job in the early 1600s. Rich folks were too busy to learn this new game, so they asked him to explore it and tell them what he found. The first chess professional, Greco got paid to study.

1. ♘g6+   hxg6
2. ♖h1#

1. ♕h5   h6

2. ♕g6   hxg5
3. ♕h5#

Chernev was the most enthusiastic cheerleader among chess authors. He said that one of his favorite games for introducing people to the beauty of chess was Anderssen-Lange, Breslau 1859, where Black's minor-piece sacrifices set up Greco's mating pattern, and although White squirmed free of that, Black's Damiano bishop (Renaud and Kahn's mate no. 12B) was a killer.

Game 32

Breslau 1859
White: Adolf Anderssen
Black: Max Lange
Ruy López

1. e4   e5
2. ♘f3   ♘c6
3. ♗b5   ♘d4
4. ♘xd4   exd4

Bird's Defense 3...♘d4 loses a move, but Black's recapture increases his space on the queenside.

5. ♗c4   ...

One of Black's ideas is to fill up the queenside with ...c7-c6 and ...d7-d5, so White moves the bishop in advance. Purdy said if you know you're going to make a move soon, it's not a bad idea to make it now.

5. ...   ♘f6

Black threatens.

6. e5   ...

White threatens.

6. ...   d5

Black threatens. This is how good players play: attack, counterattack, counter-counterattack. Anderssen and Lange were two of the best players of their day, and two of the great attacking players in history. (Chess historians aren't certain about this game's provenance. *Schachjahrbuch für 1917/18* by L. Bachmann gives the gamescore up to 13. ♖f5! as Anderssen-Dufresne, Berlin 1851.)

7. ♗b3   ♗g4

Before the f6-knight moves away from the pawn's jab, it supports the bishop's development with a greater threat. Black had to calculate well, because White's reply puts two black pieces under attack.

8. f3   ♘e4
9. 0-0   ...

Not 9. fxg4, because 9...♕h4+ starts a winning attack. Black wants to develop the king bishop aggressively, but 9...♗c5 10. d3 stifles it, so Black moved the blocking pawn out of the way first.

9. ...   d3
10. fxg4   ...

10. ♕e1 is better, guarding against knight checks on f2 and g3 following 10...♗c5+ 11. ♔h1.

10. ...   ♗c5+
11. ♔h1   ...

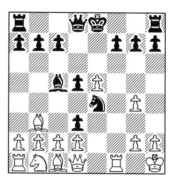

11. ...   ♘g3+!
12. hxg3   ...

Now Black's job is to deliver mate on the h-file. 12...h5 comes to mind, but a queen move introduces more new force.

12. ...   ♕g5
13. ♖f5   h5
14. gxh5   ♕xf5
15. g4   ♖xh5+

Chess history buffs tend to agree that this score is the result of analysis Anderssen and Lange performed together on Anderssen-Dufresne, Berlin 1851. That makes sense, because the more precise and thematic finish would have been 15...♕f2!, but then there wouldn't have been the neat queen-plus-bishop coordination at the end.

16. gxh5   ♕e4
17. ♕f3   ♕h4+
18. ♕h3   ♕e1+
19. ♔h2   ♗g1+
20. ♔h1   ♗f2+
21. ♔h2   ♕g1#
0-1

Game 33

New York 1906
White: Albert Whiting Fox
Black: J.R. Capablanca
Ruy López

1.	e4	e5
2.	♘f3	♘c6
3.	♗b5	♘f6
4.	0-0	♗e7
5.	♖e1	d6

This game inspired me to take up Steinitz's defense to the Ruy López, which a master equated with my desire to improve: "Capablanca played that when he was young and hungry," he said. Beware of ambition, though — that great philosopher and chessplayer Bob Dylan once said, "Basically you have to suppress your own ambitions in order to be who you need to be."

6.	d4	exd4
7.	♘xd4	♗d7
8.	♘c3	0-0

Black has developed as his compact position allowed, but now he would like to get some cars out of gridlock with two exchanges: ...♘xd4 plus ...♗xb5. White ought to avoid at least one — simplest is 9. ♗xc6, but if White decides to preserve the bishop, then 9. ♗f1 is preferable (9. ♗c4 can be attacked by ...♗e6 or ...♘e5, whereas 9. ♗e2 gums up the queen and rook).

9.	♘de2	♖e8
10.	♘g3	♘e5

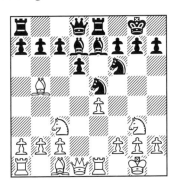

Golombek could see in this move the seeds of the "Capablanca freeing maneuver" in the Orthodox Queen's Gambit Declined: 1. d4 ♘f6 2. ♘f3 d5 3. c4 e6 4. ♘c3 ♗e7 5. ♗g5 ♘bd7 6. e3 0-0 7. ♖c1 c6 8. ♗d3 dxc4 9. ♗xc4 ♘d5, effecting two exchanges from a cramped position.

11.	♗xd7	♕xd7
12.	f4	...

Doesn't fit once White has moved his rook off the f-file. A bishop development is called for — maybe ♗g5 looking ahead to ♗xf6 so that both white knights will have strong posts at d5 or f5.

12. ...		♘g6
13. ♘f5		...

The fifth move for this knight while the queenside pieces are neglected.

13. ...		♗f8
14. ♕d3		♖ad8

Black has taken the lead in development. If he achieves better control of the center after advancing ...d6-d5, he will have the advantage.

15. ♗d2

If 15. ♗e3, then 15...d5 16. e5 as in the game, but 16...♘g4 threatens 17... ♘xe3 to remove the guard of f4 and to set up the pawn fork ...d5-d4.

15. ...	d5
16. e5	♗c5+
17. ♔h1	♘g4
18. ♘d1	...

The knight fork is prevented, but White has disconnected his rooks and fallen further behind in development. The better-developed side continues to fight for center control, and to open the position for his active pieces.

18. ...	f6!

Demolishing White's center. Capablanca described this unfolding of Greco's Mate in *My Chess Career*: 19. exf6 ♘xf4 20. ♘e7+ (otherwise the queen and knight lose contact, while White cannot counterattack the c5-bishop with 20. ♖xe8+ ♖xe8 21. ♕c3, because 21...♕xf5 22. ♕xc5 ♘e2 wins) 20...♖xe7 21. fxe7 ♘xd3 22. exd8♕+ ♕xd8 23. cxd3 ♕h4 24. h3 ♕g3! 25. hxg4 ♕h4#.

19. h3	♘f2+
20. ♘xf2	♗xf2
21. ♖e2	

Black's campaign for taking control of the center included recognizing that he could ignore this threat.

21. ...	fxe5!
22. ♖xf2	e4

Regaining the piece with a superior position.

23. ♘h6+	gxh6
24. ♕d4	♕g7

Contesting the diagonal before ♗d2-c3 becomes a bother.

25. ♕xa7	...

The queen will be separated from her army by the Black center. More stubborn was 25. ♗c3 ♕xd4 26. ♗xd4 b6 27. b4 e3 28. ♖e2 ♘xf4 29. ♖xe3 ♖e4 30. ♖g3+ ♔f7 31. c3.

25. ...	♕xb2
26. ♖e1	...

Strikes a sour note. Rooks are the worst pieces to put in front of a passed pawn, because every time the pawn advances, the rook's scope is lessened.

26. ...	d4

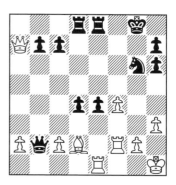

27. f5	...

27. ♗c1 is a threat Black can ignore: 27...e3! 28. ♗xb2 exf2 29. ♖f1 ♖e1 and wins.

27. ...	e3

Black is in control, and proceeds ruthlessly. 27...e3 is the first of three threatening moves in a row.

28.	🖺fe2	♞f4
29.	♝c1	♛b6
30.	♛a4	♞xe2
31.	♛c4+	♚h8
32.	🖺xe2	♛a6

32. ♛xe2 would've avoided this skewer.

33.	♛d3	♛xd3
34.	cxd3	c5

Introducing unused force with the plan of breaking the blockade.

35.	g4	c4

0-1

Game 34

La Habana 1902
White: Rafael Blanco
Black: J.R. Capablanca
Two Knights' Defense

1.	e4	e5
2.	♞f3	♞c6

Before players reach master strength, they ought to cultivate the habit of counterattacking whenever they can, starting with 2...♞f6, 2...d5 or 2...f5. An old chess teacher once said: "If (students) play 2...♞c6, they're going to have to defend for a while." Strong players are capable of defending, then recognizing the right time to counterpunch, but weak players need to practice punching as soon as possible. Even in Capablanca's earliest recorded games, he was playing 2...♞c6 (he drew game 10 of the Corzo match in 1901 with 2...♞f6, but he never played another Petroff), and it is difficult to tell people "Do as I say, not as Capablanca did."

3.	♝c4	♞f6

Black's two best chances at active play are 3...♞f6, counterattacking, and 3...♝c5, where Black's queen keeps an eye on g5. However, in case of 3...♞f6 4. ♞g5, Black can ignore the threat to f7, and play 4...♝c5!.

4.	d3	...

The "modern" move, opting to go slower than 4. d4 or 4. ♞g5. Improving players should not go slow. They should speed it up and suffer several fatal crashes, then learn to dial it back. For example, if Black had played 3...♝c5, a young player as White has to tinker a few times with 4. ♝xf7+ ♚xf7 5. ♞xe5+ ♞xe5 6. ♛h5+.

4.	...	d5

This is premature, enabling White to benefit from creeping. 4...♝e7 and 4...♝c5 are more prudent. You might say 4...d5 is a case of a young player going too fast before learning to control his speed, but Capablanca played 4...d5 in this position as late as 1913, when he was acknowledged as one of the world's preeminent masters.

5.	exd5	♞xd5
6.	0-0	♝e7
7.	🖺e1	...

The trouble with 4...d5 is that the e5-pawn comes under fire. White is better after 8. d4.

7. ...   f6
8. ♘h4   ♗e6

9. f4   ...

Black was ready to meet 9. ♕h5+ with 9...♗f7, so it was better to develop the next-most unused force with 9. ♘c3, when Black ought not be comfortable with 9...♘xc3 10. ♕h5+ ♔d7 11. ♗xe6+.

9. ...   ♘xf4
10. ♗xe6   ♘xe6
11. ♕h5+   ♔d7

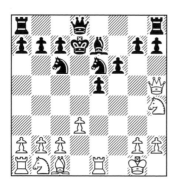

White's pawn sacrifice has resulted in the loss of Black's castling privilege, plus some confusion in Black's development, but center control has landed on Black's side of the ledger.

12. c3   ...

Covering his queen's retreat by preventing ...♘d4. Khalifman's Chess Stars team adhered to Purdy's axiom that if you know you're going to make a move soon, you should make it now: 12. ♕g4 ♗c5+ 13. ♔h1 ♗f2 14. ♖f1 h5 15. ♕c4 ♗xh4 16. ♕xh4 ♔c8, with a slight edge to Black, they said.

12. ...   g6
13. ♕f3   ...

13. ♕e2 gives the h4-knight a way home.

13. ...   ♔c8
14. d4   f5

The best way to defend, said Capablanca, is to seize the initiative. The best defense to the threatened pawn fork is a discovered counterattack.

15. ♘xf5   gxf5
16. d5   ♘ed4
17. cxd4   ♘xd4
18. ♕d3   ♗c5

When Black plays 18...♗c5, he ought to have Greco's Mate in mind: that is, 19...♘e2+ 20. ♔h1 ♘g3+ 21. hxg3 ♕h4+. In this instance, Black loses a knight and a queen, but he has to think about it.

19. ♔h1   ♕xd5

Black has stolen a second pawn and improved his position in the center. White gains two moves in development for the second pawn, but that compensation is as insufficient as for the first pawn lost.

20. ♘c3   ♛e6
21. ♗f4   e4
22. ♛h3   b6

A logical move. Black must find a way to develop his queen rook, while ...b6 shores up the loose bishop on c5.

23. ♖ac1   ♚b7
24. b4   ...

White is playing too desperately.

At move 27, he'll find two pieces attacked.

24. ...   ♗xb4
25. ♘xe4   fxe4
26. ♖xc7+   ♚a6
27. g4   ♗xe1
28. ♛f1+   b5
29. ♛xe1   ♛xg4

Suddenly White's king is in greater danger than Black's. The threat of ...♛f3+ plus ...♘e2+ forces the queens off the board, after which White's counterplay is kaput.

30. ♛f2   ♛f3+
31. ♛xf3   ♘xf3
0-1

Chapter 11

Anastasia's Mate

Anastasia's Mate is so pretty and rare, but it landed in the "Typical Mates" section of *The Art of the Checkmate* instead of "Picturesque Mates." Maybe Renaud and Kahn ran afoul of a Dilbertian pointy-haired editor in 1953.

1.	♘e7+	♚h8
2.	♕xh7+	♚xh7
3.	♖h1#	

White: Garfield
Black: Heathcliff
Bishop's Opening

1.	e4	e5
2.	♗c4	♘f6
3.	♘c3	♗b4
4.	♘ge2	♘xe4
5.	0-0	...

White probably elected against 5. ♘xe4 d5 because he wanted to make 4. ♘ge2 a useful move.

5. ...	♘xc3

In a 1917 Argentinian correspondence game, Schindler played 5...♘f6 against Theiler, and won in 21 moves.

6. ♘xc3	...

6. dxc3 is better because it threatens, and frees the queenside, but 6. ♘xc3 is consistent with ♘ge2.

6.	...	0-0
7.	♖e1	d5?
8.	♘xd5	♗a5
9.	♖xe5	c6
10.	♘e7+	♚h8
11.	♕h5!	♗c7
12.	♕xh7+	♚xh7
13.	♖h5#	1-0

Game 35

Margate 1936
White: J.R. Capablanca
Black: Vera Menchik
Queen's Gambit Declined

1.	d4	d5
2.	♘f3	♘f6

3. c4   c5

Writers remember their earliest published pieces. I wrote about this symmetrical defense in Seirawan's games from the 1992 Melody Amber tournament for the *Golden Gate Chess News*. Play can proceed like a Tarrasch Defense, or a Queen's Gambit Accepted, and sometimes it goes its own way.

4. cxd5   cxd4

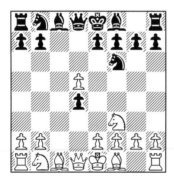

5. ♘xd4   ...

Black might equalize more easily if the queens come off: 5. ♕xd4 ♕xd5 6. ♘c3 ♕xd4 7. ♘xd4. Then it helps to be cautious with 7...a6; the provocative 7...e5 8. ♘db5 ♔d8 led to a loss for Black in Lasker-Tarrasch, Berlin 1916.

5. ...   ♘xd5
6. e4   ...

White took a simple route to an opening advantage. Black has to move the knight a third time, while White has the only pawn in the center.

6. ...   ♘b4

The black knights cooperate, so that if 7. ♗b5+, 7...♘4c6 or 7...♘8c6 are safe interpositions. The attacking move 6...♘f6 leads to 7. ♘c3 e5

8. ♗b5+, an open position in which White has an edge in development and is closer to castling.

7. ♗e3   ...

7. ♕a4+, forking, is the biggest threat by the biggest unused piece. After 7...♘8c6, the d4-knight hangs, so 8. ♘xc6 ♘xc6 9. ♘c3 with a slight advantage for White.

7. ...   a6

This can't be right. 7...♘8c6 develops with the threat 8...♘xd4 9. ♗xd4 ♕xd4 10. ♕xd4 ♘c2+.

8. ♕a4+   ♘4c6

The women's world champion lost all nine of her tournament games against Capablanca. Moves like 8...♘4c6 are to blame because 8...♘8c6, using inactive force, was available.

9. ♘c3   e6
10. ♘db5   ...

White has better center control and is three moves ahead in development, but goes weirdly afield. 10. ♖d1 is a developing move with a threat.

10. ...   ♘d7
11. ♖d1   ...

The bug in the program is that 12. ♘d6+ is a threat that Black can ignore. Capablanca retired from tournament chess between New York 1931 and Hastings 1935, and Golombek said even before 1931 "errors became more frequent, while the old, calm, clear, harmonious style is no longer to be seen except for brief moments." Capablanca enjoyed a resurgence in 1936 — two first places at Moscow and Nottingham, and second at Margate.

11. ...   ♖b8

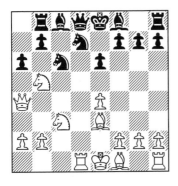

12. ♘d4 ...

White also loses a bit of his lead with 12. ♘d6+ ♗xd6 13. ♖xd6 ♕c7. In any event, Black relieves some of her constriction by exchanging.

12. ... ♘xd4
13. ♕xd4 ♕f6
14. ♕c4 ...

14. ♕a7 threatened 15. ♖xd7.

14. ... ♗e7
15. f4 ...

That's more like it. White grabs more of the center, and has the plan of reaching d6 by e4-e5 and ♘e4-d6.

15. ... ♗d8
16. e5 ♕h4+
17. g3 ♕e7
18. ♘e4 ♗a5+
19. ♔f2 0-0
20. ♘d6 ♗b6

Black is still trying to get some pieces off the gridlocked side of the chessboard, but is swapping good bishop for bad.

21. ♗xb6 ♘xb6
22. ♕d4 ♘d5
23. ♗g2 ♗d7
24. ♗xd5 ..

Played before Black can play ... ♗c6 to preserve her structure. The d6-knight becomes the boss minor piece, dominating the bishop that is already blocked by black pawns.

24. ... exd5
25. ♖he1 ...

To cobble together a couple of general principles, White's unused rook belongs behind a potentially passed pawn.

25. ... ♗c6

26. ♘f5

Black has to be careful. For instance, the rooks run out of mobility after 26...♕d8 27. e6 ♕f6 28. ♕xf6 gxf6 29. e7 plus 30. ♘d6.

26. ... ♕e6
27. g4 ♖bc8
28. h3 ...

Relieving a pin on the knight.

28. ... ♖c7
29. ♕b6 ...

Threatening, while Black is barred from doubling on the file because 29... ♖fc8 30. ♘d6 drives off the guard.

29. ... ♖cc8
30. ♔g3 ...

Allowing no hint of counterplay, whereas Black gets clues from the move order 30. ♘d4 ♕g6 31. f5 ♕h6.

30. ...   d4

That's the right idea: the d5-pawn did more harm than good, so Black ejects it.

31. ♖xd4   ♖ce8

30...d4 to free the bishop was good thinking, but this is another lifeless move. Black could not yet play 31...♗d5 because of 32. ♕xe6 plus 33. ♘e7+, so perhaps 31...♔h8 is indicated before ...♗d5 and then ...♖fd8.

32. b3   h5
33. ♖d6   ♕c8
34. ♕d4   ...

Black would have been grateful for 34. ♖ed1 ♗e4.

34. ...   ♖e6
35. ♖xe6   ♕xe6
36. ♕d6   hxg4

The position reduces to a win for White on 36...♕xd6 37. exd6 hxg4 38. ♘e7+ ♔h7 39. hxg4 ♖d8 40. ♖d1 (not 40. ♖e2 to threaten Anastasia's Mate because 40...♖xd6 enables Black's useful interposition ...♖h6) g6 41. ♘xc6 bxc6 42. f5 followed by ♔f4.

37. ♘e7+   ♔h7
38. ♕xe6   fxe6
39. hxg4   ♖d8
40. ♔h4   ...

Perhaps evoking the same active king from Capablanca-Tartakover, New York 1924.

40. ...   ♗f3

41. ♔g5   ...

White's king is actively placed and sheltered from the enemy rook. White threatens 42. ♖e3 ♗g2 43. ♖e2, winning the bishop or delivering Anastasia's Mate.

41. ...   ♖d7
42. ♘g6   ♖d2

White threatened a fork on f8, but 42...♔g8 runs into 43. ♖e3 ♗g2 44. ♖e2 ♗c6 45. ♖h2 plus ♖h8 and ♖f8#, kind of a cousin to the Arabian Mate.

43. ♖c1   ♗c6
44. ♘f8+   ♔g8
45. ♘xe6   ♖xa2
46. ♘d4   ♗b5
47. ♖c8+   ♔h7

47...♔f7 48. e6+ ♔e7 49. ♖c7+ ♔d8 50. ♘xb5 axb5 51. ♖xg7 is a bulldozer for White.

48. ♘e6   1-0

Black gave up in view of 49. ♘f8+ ♔g8 50. ♘g6+ ♔f7 51. f5 with mate to follow.

Chapter 12

Boden's Mate

Studies of pattern recognition in human chessplayers have found that humans identify some checkmating sequences faster than computers do. The researchers pointed to this study by Damiano, which experienced players recognize before their eyes take in the entire picture.

Study by Damiano, 1512

1.	♖h8+	♔xh8
2.	♖h1+	♔g8
3.	♖h8+	♔xh8
4.	♕h1+	♔g8
5.	♕h7#	

Similarly, when a chessplayer leafs through a book of puzzles and spots a black king behind the Caro-Slav pawn structure plus a white bishop on f4, he might turn the page before looking for the other elements of Boden's Mate.

1.	♕xc6+	bxc6
2.	♗a6#	

Game 36

Budapest 1934
White: Esteban Canal
Black: A.N. Other
Scandinavian Defense

1.	e4	d5
2.	exd5	♕xd5
3.	♘c3	♕a5
4.	d4	c6
5.	♘f3	♗g4
6.	♗f4	e6
7.	h3	♗xf3
8.	♕xf3	♗b4
9.	♗e2	♘d7
10.	a3	0-0-0?

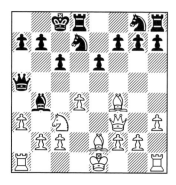

If White recognizes the Boden's Mate pattern, he'll follow this positional logic: If I can deflect the black queen's attention from a6, I can checkmate.

11. axb4! ♕xa1+
12. ♔d2! ♕xh1

12. ♔d2! discovered the threat 13. ♖xa1 when the queen has no safe retreat along the a-file. After 12...♕xh1, a6 is safe for the bishop.

13. ♕xc6+! bxc6
14. ♗a6# 1-0

A briefer example, but not as flashy: Cardiff-Bristol, correspondence 1969: 1. e4 e5 2. f4 d5 3. exd5 e4 4. ♗b5+ c6 5. dxc6 bxc6 6. ♗a4 ♕d4 7. c3 ♕d6 8. ♘e2 ♗g4 9. 0-0 ♕d3 10. ♖e1 ♗c5+ 11. ♔f1 ♕f3+! 12. gxf3 ♗h3# 0-1.

Game 37

Buenos Aires 1911
White: A. Israel
Black: J.R. Capablanca
Caro-Kann Defense

1. e4 c6

It's ironic that Black opened with the Caro-Kann Defense because it is the Caro-Slav formations that often fall to Boden's Mate.

2. d4 d5
3. ♘c3 dxe4
4. ♘xe4 ♗f5

4...♘f6 also develops with a threat, and then 5. ♘xf6+ exf6 frees the king bishop, while 5...gxf6 captures toward the center with potential for using the g-file.

5. ♘g3 ♗g6
6. ♗c4 ...

In modern practice, White often gains as much time and space as he can by chasing the black bishop: 6. h4 h6 7. ♘f3 ♘d7 8. h5 ♗h7 9. ♗d3 ♗xd3 10. ♕xd3.

6. ... ♘d7
7. ♘1e2 ...

This maneuver is more effective with the interpolation of 7. h4 h6, because ♘e2-f4 would then make a serious positional threat of ♘xg6.

7. ... e6
8. ♘f4 ♘gf6

But while the black pawn is on h7, Black can ignore the threat ♘xg6 because ...hxg6 activates the rook for free.

9. c3 ♗d6
10. ♕e2 ♕c7

Developing with a threat. White had a change of heart about 11. ♘xg6 because 11...hxg6 threatens 12...♗xg3 13. fxg3 ♖xh2! 14. ♖xh2 ♕xg3+.

11. ♘d3 0-0-0
12. ♗d2 e5

The time White wasted on three knight moves enabled Black to nose ahead in development, and having achieved the pawn break ...e6-e5, Black has equal control of the center.

13. dxe5	**♞xe5**
14. ♞xe5	**♝xe5**
15. 0-0-0	**♛a5**

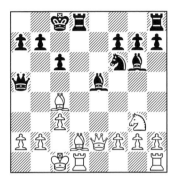

15...♛a5 neither uses inactive force nor makes a threat (15...♜he8 would do both). This game is here because Black's reply to 15. 0-0-0 was to immediately put his queen in place for the Boden's Mate pattern.

One should almost never go without a plan at the chessboard if one knows some checkmating patterns — one can imagine the checkmate that is closest to the position at hand, and maneuver the pieces toward that checkmate.

16. f4	**♝d6**

Imagination has its place at the chessboard. Suppose White plays 17. ♝e3. Then Black could play 17...♜he8 to threaten 18...♝xf4, and if White breaks that pin by 18. ♛f3, then Black springs Boden's Mate by 18...♛xc3+ 19. bxc3 ♝a3#.

That would've been much more interesting than what actually happened. White lost time while exchanging into an even endgame, tangled the two pieces he had left, mobilized the wrong one, and then didn't attack with it when he had the chance.

17. f5	**♝xf5**

18. ♞xf5	**♛xf5**
19. ♝xf7	**...**

If White were more interested in gathering his forces than in grabbing a pawn, 19. ♜hf1 ♛d7 20. ♝g5 ♜he8 21. ♛f3 ♛c7 22. ♝xf6 gxf6 23. g3 looks headed for a draw.

19. ...	**♚c7**
20. ♜hf1	**♛e4**
21. ♛xe4	**...**

White might think he's getting closer to the draw by winding up with a bishop against a knight in the ending, but the truth of the position is that Black gets two active pieces against none. 21. ♛f2 threatens, and doesn't bring a black piece up.

21. ...	**♞xe4**
22. ♝f4	**...**

It would be hard for either side to win after 22. g3, but White loses time by bringing black pieces up to d6.

22. ...	**♜hf8**
23. ♝xd6+	**♜xd6**
24. ♜xd6	**♚xd6**

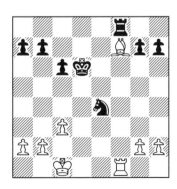

25. ♝c4	**...**

Another ill-judged simplification. White's pieces are more active after 25. ♜d1+ ♚c7 26. ♝b3 ♜f2 27. ♝c2.

25. ...	♖xf1+
26. ♗xf1	♔e5
27. ♔d1	...

Black is ahead only slightly after 27. ♗d3. White's next two king moves quite hinder his bishop. In endgames of bishops against knights, one of the bishop's most important tasks is to limit the movements of the knight, but White took poor care of his bishop in this game.

27. ...	♔f4
28. ♔e2	h5

29. ♔d3   ...

White might have counted on 29. g3+, but Black is winning after 29... ♘xg3+ 30. hxg3+ ♔xg3 31. ♔e3 g5 32. ♗e2 h4. White should probably activate his bishop before his king with 29. ♔e1 ♔e3 30. ♗c4. When a piece has to be assigned a defensive duty (like holding the kingside), the smallest piece possible ought to be left behind so the bigger pieces can attack. If 29. ♔e1 and 30. ♗c4, the bishop can influence the kingside battle from the rear as the king meets it head on, while

the bishop can attack the queenside through e6 and c8.

29. ...	g5
30. ♗e2	g4
31. b4	h4
32. ♔d4	♘g5
33. a4	g3
34. hxg3+	♔xg3
35. ♔e5	♔xg2
36. ♗g4	♔g3
37. ♗c8	♘f7+
38. ♔d4	...

White could play more aggressively with his king: 38. ♔f6 ♘d6 39. ♗e6 h3 40. ♗xh3 ♔xh3 41. ♔e6, but Black's king brings help in time: 41...♘e4 42. c4 ♔g4.

38. ...	♘d6
39. ♗d7	h3
40. ♗xh3	♔xh3
41. c4	♔g4
42. c5	♘f7
43. b5	♔f5
44. ♔c4	♔e4
45. a5	♘e5+
46. ♔b4	a6
0-1	

Chapter 13

Mate no. 8

1.	e4	c5
2.	♘f3	♘c6
3.	d4	cxd4
4.	♘xd4	♘f6
5.	♘c3	e5

When it comes to the naming of openings, moves or sequences have logically taken on the names of people, places, or things: the players who first played or analyzed or popularized them, the places where they were invented or figured prominently, or things they resemble in some fashion (like "spikes" or "dragons").

The best-known player to try this Sicilian variation was a world champion early in the 20th century. Then a couple of Argentinian grandmasters developed its theory in the 1950s, while the variation was revolutionized by a couple of grandmasters from Byelorussia in the late 1970s. But the chess community couldn't

decide whether to rename the opening after its greatest adherents or their hometown, so this Sicilian line sometimes goes by the name Lasker-Pilnik-Pelikan-Chelyabinsk-Sveshnikov Variation, while some practical types call it "one of those ugly things with the huge hole on d5."

The hole, incidentally, has a name. The Soviet grandmaster Boleslavsky, one of the top players in mid-century, helped prove that Black's dynamic potential in the center — where he has one more pawn, after all — was worth taking on the huge positional liability that became known as the Boleslavsky Hole.

Renaud and Kahn did important work in 1953, giving names to some endgame patterns in the same way openings got names. For instance, Greco and Damiano analyzed some checkmates first, so those bear their names, while the smothered and *épaulettes* mates describe themselves.

However, when Renaud and Kahn got to some common themes against castled positions, they didn't think any single player deserved credit, while the mating patterns themselves weren't evocative of an interesting nomenclature. So they sort of dropped the ball on a couple of checkmates in *The Art of the Checkmate*. This queen-plus-pawn coordination is called simply, Mate no. 8:

With White to play, Mate no. 8 is an easy matter:

1. f6   1-0

It's more interesting with Black on the move. This pattern is known as Lolli's Mate:

1. ...   ♔h8
2. f6   g6

Or 2...gxf6 3. ♕xf6+ ♔g8 4. ♖g3#.

3. ♕h6   ♖g8
4. ♕xh7+ ...

Lolli's Mate is fun to explore because there are variations on the theme. In positions where 4. ♕xh7+ doesn't fetch, sometimes the pinning/deflecting move 4. ♖a8 is the key, or the direct 4. ♖h3.

4. ...   ♔xh7
5. ♖h3#

Game 38

New York 1906
White: J.R. Capablanca
Black: Robert Raubitschek
Ruy López

1. e4   ...

Games collections authored by the player himself have one exceptional

thing going for them: he thinks they are his best games. Even though Capablanca thought this game suitable for *My Chess Career*, I didn't think so highly of it in the past. In fact, I didn't consider it for this book until the first draft was complete.

But one of the best reasons for progressing at chess is being able to understand more clearly the moves of others as well as one's own. I find now — after years of slow improvement — that I appreciate how smoothly Capablanca carried this game from opening to ending.

The lesson of the story is: If you are young, study harder than I did when I was a kid. Get good while study time is available. Nothing squashes an adult's growth at chess flatter than adult responsibilities.

1. ...   e5
2. ♘f3   ♘c6
3. ♗b5   ♘f6
4. 0-0   ♘xe4
5. d4   d5

5...d5 gives the b5-bishop pinning power, and then White's capture on e5 hits the pinned piece. Kramnik won a world championship match partly because his 5...♘d6 6. ♗xc6 dxc6 7. dxe5 ♘f5 defense proved so ornery.

6. ♘xe5   ♗d7
7. ♘xd7   ♕xd7
8. ♘c3   ...

Developing with a threat to threaten by 9. ♖e1.

8. ...   f5

Black falls behind permanently after this move, which neglects his development and weakens his king's position. White's advantage is narrower after 8...♘xc3 9. bxc3 ♗e7 10. ♖e1 0-0

11. ♖b1, when he has open lines for his long-range pieces and possibilities on both wings following the discovered attack 12. ♗d3.

9. ♘xe4   fxe4

White's reply makes the most direct hit to Black's center, including the threat 11. ♕h5+.

10. c4   ...

The most important suggestion Capablanca made in his writings was that, "the student should work this out," which should apply to every note, not just those which say so explicitly.

I spent the longest night in a library ascertaining an errant note in *Chess Fundamentals*, which proved that when Capablanca wrote "the student should work this out," he really meant it. Never trust anything you read in chess books.

In *My Chess Career*, Capablanca offers this alternative to 10. c4: 10. ♗xc6 bxc6 11. ♕h5+ ♕f7 12. ♕xf7+ ♔xf7 13. f3 exf3 14. ♖xf3+ ♔e6 15. ♗g5 c5 16. ♖e1+ ♔d7 17. ♖f7+ ♔c6 "and White has a slight advantage." But doesn't White's lead in development plus Black's pawn weaknesses suggest more than a slight edge? For instance, 18. ♗f4 ♖c8 19. ♖e6+ ♔b5 20. ♖d7.

10. ...   0-0-0

White's next few moves have the feel of effortlessness that was Capablanca's trademark.

11. ♗g5   ♗e7
12. ♗xe7   ♕xe7
13. ♗xc6   bxc6
14. c5   ...

By closing the center, White stakes all on reaching the enemy king before Black does. Purdy wrote that, "in games of opposite castling, sacrifice anything but time."

14. ...   ♕f6
15. ♕a4   ...

White based his decision at move 14 on the relative weaknesses in the kings' fields. The holes and immobile pawns in Black's position enable White to find threats.

15. ...   ♔b8
16. ♖ac1   ...

Players mostly get frantic in these positions, flinging pieces and pawns forward without anything specific in mind. 16. ♖ac1 starts a rather orderly sequence aimed at advancing c5 to c6 to take over the b7-square.

16. ...   ♔a8
17. b4   ♖b8
18. a3   ♖he8
19. ♕a6   ♖e6

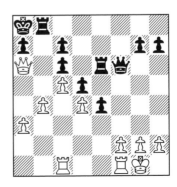

20. a4   ...

The other comment Purdy had about games with castling on opposite wings is that, "it is blessedly better to give than receive."

20. ...   ♕xd4

If 20...♖xb4, then 21. ♖b1 conquers the b-file for White's pieces.

21. b5   ♕f6
22. ♖c2   ...

White's plan is 23. ♖b1, followed by 24. ♖cb2 and 25. bxc6.

22. ...   cxb5
23. c6   b4

Black succeeded in keeping the b-file closed, but White maneuvers around the b4-pawn.

24. ♖c5   ♕d4
25. ♖b5   ♖ee8
26. ♖b7   ♕c5
27. h3   d4

28. ♔h2   ...

An important *luft* move. If Black doesn't capture the white rook with check, then White can make attacking decoy moves with his rook.

28. ...   d3
29. ♖c1!   ♕xf2?

Capablanca said Black's only chance was 29...♕d4 30. ♖c4 ♕b6 31. ♖xb6 ♖xb6 32. ♖xe4 ♖xe4 33. ♕c8+ ♖b8 34. ♕xc7 with a difficult game. 29...♕xf2 enables White to lift another rook to the mating net.

30. ♖f1!   ♕d4
31. ♖f5   ...

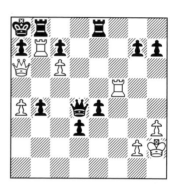

31. ...   e3

31...♕b6 32. ♖xa7+ ♕xa7 33. ♖a5 ♕xa5 34. ♖xa5# is a form of Lolli's Mate.

32. ♖a5   ♕f4+
33. ♔g1   ♕d4
34. ♖xa7+   ♕xa7
35. ♕xa7#   1-0

Game 39

Prague 1911
White: J. Podhajsky
Black: J.R. Capablanca
Dutch Defense

1. d4   f5

Capablanca usually chose the sounder 1...♘f6 2. c4 e6 3. ♘c3 ♗b4, and then when the time was right, ...♘e4 plus ...f7-f5 to reach the same kind of position.

2. c4 ...

A perfectly good move, but if White wants to take the rumble right into Black's neighborhood, then 2. e4 aims for the quickest development while Black's king position is weakened and his development lags.

2. ... e6
3. ♘c3 ♘f6
4. ♗f4 ...

Some developing moves are lifeless. The pivotal square is e4 — excellent development schemes against the Dutch include g2-g3 and ♗f1-g2, with the e2-e4 advance on the horizon. Since e2-e4 is so vital, then 4. ♗g5 would have been better, assuming White felt compelled to move his bishop.

4. ... ♗b4
5. e3 ...

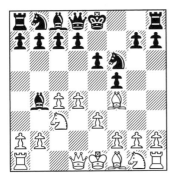

5. ... 0-0

At the 2008 Reykjavík Open, Persson went for the full Nimzo-Indian approach against Kjartansson — crippling the c-pawns before immobilizing and killing them — with 5...♗xc3+.

6. ♗e2 ...

Another humdrum development. 6. ♗d3 goes more to the heart of the position, while Hort-Grynszpan, Lugano

1989, saw immediate skirmishing: 6. ♘e2 ♘e4 7. h4 b6 8. ♕b3 a5.

6. ... ♘c6

It could be imagined that if Black were less careful in his move order, then White might be inspired to put his minor pieces on better squares: 6... b6 7. ♗f3 ♘c6 8. ♘e2.

7. ♘f3 ...

Had White played 6. ♗d3, he could have developed the knight to e2, enabling his pawns to eventually inch up with f2-f3 plus e3-e4.

7. ... b6
8. h3 ...

One of several reasons for useless P-R3 moves is to make *luft* for a bishop, when Black is simply not going to play ...♘h5. Also, if White determines later that he wants to evict a black knight from e4, he will be reluctant to play f2-f3, because that would make Swiss cheese out of his castled formation.

8. ... ♗b7
9. 0-0 ♘e4

White perceives a choice of evils. He can allow the doubling of his c-pawns by ...♗xc3, after which Black can attack the c4-pawn with moves like ...♘a5 and ...♗a6. Or he can swap on e4, when ...fxe4 puts a cramping pawn in White's middle, and the f-file is open for business.

Perhaps White judged 10. ♘xe4 a lesser evil because it avoids a doubled pawn while giving one to Black, and maybe the pawn on e4 will be a nuisance to the b7-bishop. Then Black has the objective of reopening the bishop's diagonal — many outstanding chess games are based on extending the scope of Dragon or Indian bishops.

10. ♘xe4   fxe4

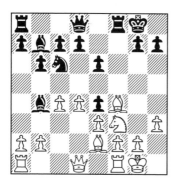

11. ♘g5   ...

The more central 11. ♘d2 has the tactical flaw 11...♘xd4 12. exd4 ♖xf4.

11. ...   ♘e7

12. ♘xe4 was not a threat to be ignored because the black pawn restricts White's pieces (for now, the knight on g5 has no safe square), but if White persists with 12. ♕c2, then Black might opt to ignore the renewed threat to make a threat of his own: 12... ♘g6 13. ♘xe4 ♘xf4 14. exf4 ♖xf4, when Black's pieces have sprung to life.

12. a3   ...

A good move, but not for the reason White thinks.

12. ...   ♗d6
13. ♗xd6   cxd6

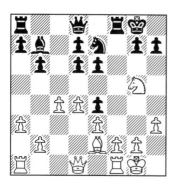

14. h4   ...

With 13. ♗xd6, White gave Black another set of doubled pawns, but the truly important detail is that Black can't attack the bishop anymore. If White threatens with 14. ♕c2, 14... ♘g6 is no longer a counterattack, and Black would hate to play 14...d5 because the b7-bishop becomes a big pawn.

14. ...   ♘f5

We could sniff that White's failure to develop 14. ♕c2 with a threat enabled Black to develop with a threat, but h2-h4 and ...♘f5 were going to happen anyway: 14. ♕c2 d5 15. cxd5 exd5 16. ♕b3 (threatening 17. ♘xe4) ♔h8 17. h4 ♘f5. We'll revisit this.

15. g3   h6
16. ♘h3   ♘xh4
17. gxh4   ♕xh4
18. ♘f4   ♖f5

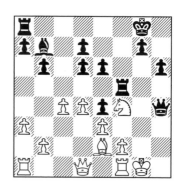

Back at move 14, Black's sacrificial line would not have a chance because there was a fork on g6: 14. ♕c2 d5 15. cxd5 exd5 16. ♕b3 ♔h8 17. h4 ♘f5 18. g3 h6 19. ♘h3 ♘xh4 20. gxh4 ♕xh4 21. ♘f4 ♖f5 22. ♘g6+. White would've done better to develop with a threat.

19. ♘h5   ...

Wasting time. It is paradoxical but better to spring the b7-bishop: 19. ♘g2 blocks the g-file, and then 19...♖g5 20. f4 exf3 21. ♗xf3, when White's bishop improves with a threat, while the f1-rook is also improved.

19. ...   ♖g5+
20. ♘g3   ♖f8

Introducing the last undeveloped piece with the huge threat of 21...♖xg3+ 22. fxg3 ♛xg3+ 23. ♔h1 ♖f3!, winning.

21. ♛e1   ♖f3

Renewing the threat to crash in on g3, and if 22. ♗xf3 exf3, Mate no. 8 follows.

22. ♔g2   ♛g4

It makes no difference whether Black plays ...♛g4 now or after White plays ♖h1, but if there's a move you are certain to play soon, it's rarely wrong to make it immediately.

23. ♖h1   h5

Besides evading the rook, the other reason for ...♛g4 was to make room for the introduction of new force.

24. ♖h3   h4
25. ♗xf3   exf3+
26. ♔h2   hxg3+

27. fxg3

Not 27. ♖xg3, for Black mates after 27...♛h4+ 28. ♔g1 ♖h5.

27. ...   f2

Which piece do you prefer, the rook on a1 or the bishop on b7?

28. ♛xf2   ♖f5

The neat *Zwischenzug* — in English, "in-between move" — nudges the queen from her guard of h4. If Black plays 28...♖h5 prematurely, then White can answer 29. ♖h4.

29. ♛d2   ...

If White tries to keep in touch with h4, the b7-bishop roars: 29. ♛e1 ♖h5 30. ♖h4 (the black pieces also cooperate well on 30. ♛f1 ♖xh3+ 31. ♛xh3 ♛e2+ 32. ♔g1 ♛xe3+) ♖xh4+ 31. gxh4 ♛g2#.

29. ...   ♖h5
30. ♖h4   ...

30. ♛g2 ♖xh3+ 31. ♛xh3 ♛e2+ as above.

30. ...   ♖xh4+
31. gxh4   ♛xh4+
0-1

32. ♔g1 ♛h1+ wins the rook.

The miniature Colle-Delvaux, Ghent 1929, shares an opening theme with Capablanca-Spielmann, New York 1927, and the key middlegame pattern with Capablanca-Jaffe, New York 1910, and Capablanca-Scott, Hastings 1919.

Game 40

Ghent 1929
White: Edgar Colle
Black: Delvaux
Colle System

1.	d4	♘f6
2.	♘f3	e6
3.	e3	d5

In *Logical Chess, Move by Move*, Chernev gives the simpler move order 1. d4 d5 2. ♘f3 ♘f6 3. e3 e6. Chess teachers learn that lessons don't require that pieces be on the precise squares, or that move orders be rigid (or even legal).

4.	♗d3	c5
5.	c3	♘c6
6.	♘bd2	♗e7
7.	0-0	...

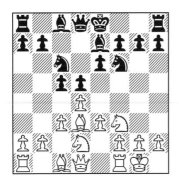

| 7. | ... | c4 |

Black gains some space on the queenside, but he lessens his influence in the center, making it easier for White to achieve the e3-e4 advance. If Black castles, White cannot play 8. e4 dxe4 9. ♘xe4 cxd4, losing a pawn, so White often plays 8. dxc5 (or 8. ♕e2 and 9. dxc5) before advancing e2-e4.

| 8. | ♗c2 | b5? |

Black's queenside motion is more weakening than threatening, exposing his c6-knight to a combination.

| 9. | e4 | dxe4 |

If White plays 10. e5, the central pawn wall cuts Black's pieces off

from defending the kingside, so he exchanges on e4, but that is an indictment of his queenside action — a player attacking on a wing should wish for a closed center, but here Black cannot accept that.

| 10. | ♘xe4 | 0-0 |
| 11. | ♕e2 | ... |

Black's loosening of his queenside enabled White to develop with the threat 12. ♘xf6+ ♗xf6 13. ♕e4, forking.

| 11. | ... | ♗b7 |
| 12. | ♘fg5 | ... |

The threat is now 13. ♘xf6+ ♗xf6 14. ♗xh7+.

12.	...	h6
13.	♘xf6+	♗xf6
14.	♕e4	g6

14...♖e8 15. ♕h7+ ♔f8 was safer than weakening the pawn shelter.

15.	♘xe6!	fxe6
16.	♕xg6+	♗g7
17.	♕h7+	...

17. ♗xh6 is not as forcing.

17.	...	♔f7
18.	♗g6+	♔f6
19.	♗h5	...

Intending 20. ♕g6+, separating black king and bishop.

| 19. | ... | ♘e7 |
| 20. | ♗xh6 | ... |

White arranged ♗xh6 for when Black's major pieces could not step up to defend the second rank, so 21. ♕xg7+ ♔f5 22. ♕e5# is threatened.

| 20. | ... | ♖g8 |
| 21. | h4 | ... |

Introducing new force with the threat 22. ♗g5#.

21. ...	♗xh6

21...e5 22. ♗xg7+ ♖xg7 23. dxe5+ ♔e6 24. ♕xg7 is also resignable for Black.

22. ♕f7#	1-0

Game 41

New York 1927
White: J.R. Capablanca
Black: Rudolf Spielmann
Queen's Gambit Declined

1. d4	...

In 1976, I was a junior high school student interested in computers when the Northwestern University program *Chess 4.5* won the Class B prize at a tournament conducted at a Silicon Valley winery. Twenty-one years later, a computer won a match from the best chessplayer in history. I cheered each development along the way, but when chess analysis software started adding prose to its annotations, I was dubious — chess annotation needs a certain *je ne sais quoi*.

One of these notes to Capablanca-Spielmann, New York 1927, was generated by *Fritz* software. Can you tell which?

1. ...	d5
2. ♘f3	e6
3. c4	♘d7

With 3...♘d7, Black tries to duck the pin that follows 3...♘f6 4. ♗g5, so that instead of ...♗e7 to break the pin, he might play more actively with the bishop by ...♗b4. Black is successful with both parts of that scheme infrequently.

4. ♘c3	♘gf6
5. ♗g5	♗b4

The Vienna Variation of Ragozin's Defense to the Queen's Gambit. Another way to reach this position was through the Leningrad Variation of the Nimzo-Indian: 1. d4 ♘f6 2. c4 e6 3. ♘c3 ♗b4 4. ♗g5 d5 5. ♘f3 ♘bd7. It's less important to know the names of things than it is to understand that it's a sharp position in which Black can pressure the dark squares.

6. cxd5	...

If 6. e3 so the bishop can retake on c4, then 6...c5 makes a positional threat to isolate the d4-pawn, and White might feel compelled to play 7. cxd5 anyway.

6. ...	exd5
7. ♕a4	...

Now if 7...c5 8. e3, it's the d5-pawn that will be isolated.

7. ...	♗xc3+
8. bxc3	...

If 8...h6, White should prefer 9. ♗xf6 ♕xf6 10. e3 to 9. ♗h4 g5 10. ♗g3 ♘e4, where Black pokes at the dark squares.

8. ...	0-0

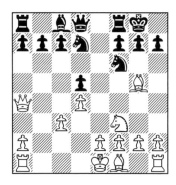

9. e3   c5

9...h6 is an important move for untangling the black kingside (without it, Black later on took two moves to play ...♕e7-e6). Then 10. ♗h4 c5 11. ♗d3 c4 12. ♗c2 g5 13. ♗g3 ♘b6 14. ♕b4 ♘e4 15. ♗xe4 dxe4 is similar to Capablanca-Spielmann, except that Black's knight can become centralized on d5.

After 16. ♘d2 ♘d5 in Romanov-Fressinet, 2009 European Championship, White got grubby with 17. ♕xc4, and Black's pieces were swiftly active with 17...♗e6 18. ♕b5 ♘xc3 19. ♕xb7 ♕b6 20. ♕xb6 axb6. Black won in 34 moves.

10. ♗d3   c4

A greatly committal move, giving up Black's pressure on the center, and betting entirely on his queenside motion. 10...c4 also immobilizes the black pawns, and White's e3-e4 advance will hit the structure at its base, exposing c4 as a target while freeing the white pieces.

11. ♗c2   ♕e7
12. 0-0   a6
13. ♖fe1   ...

Threatening to play 14. e4 with an excellent position.

13. ...   ♕e6
14. ♘d2   b5
15. ♕a5   ♘e4
16. ♘xe4   ...

White terminates the opponent with strong threats.

16. ...   dxe4

Compared to Romanov-Fressinet in the note at move 9, Black is further behind in development, and his queenside pawns are weaker. White attacks the queenside pawns immediately.

17. a4   ...

Introducing two inactive units with a threatening move.

17. ...   ♕d5

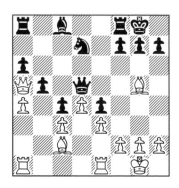

If Black's threat affords him the time to play 18...♗b7, his position isn't too bad.

18. axb5!   ...

White asked himself what if he ignored the threat to the bishop, and saw his queenside initiative turning into a storm.

18. ...   ♕xg5
19. ♗xe4   ♖b8

Black isn't helped by 19...♖a7 20. b6 ♕xa5 21. bxa7 ♕xa1 22. ♖xa1 ♘b6 23. ♖b1.

20. bxa6   ♖b5

20...♕xa5 21. ♖xa5 ♗xa6 22. ♖xa6 is tantamount to giving up.

21. ♕c7   ♘b6
22. a7   ...

22. ♖eb1 did not threaten.

22. ...   ♗h3

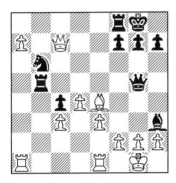

23. ♖eb1   ...

Because of ...♗h3, 23. ♖eb1 threatens 24. ♖xb5 ♕xb5 25. gxh3.

23. ...   ♖xb1+
24. ♖xb1   f5
25. ♗f3   ...

25. ♕c5 was also very good, but not 25. ♕xb6?, when a relative of Mate no. 8 follows 25...fxe4.

25. ...   f4

White's position is secure enough to handle Mate no. 8 in the air: 25...♗xg2 26. ♗xg2 f4 27. ♖xb6 f3 28. ♕g3.

26. exf4   1-0

Smiting the e6-f7-g6 Pawn Structure

The nature of the e6-f7-g6 pawn triangle in the diagram is that no matter which piece White throws at it — ♗xe6, ♘xf7, or ♘xg6 — Black's recapture results in the pawn structure e6-g6-h6, an unsatisfactory shelter for the king partly because the shield is too far from the body and because the pawns are themselves so weak.

The e6-f7 structure arises in dozens of openings — French, Caro-Kann and Slav, Catalan, Scandinavian, Blackmar-Diemer, Alekhine, Torre, Queen's Gambits accepted and declined, some Sicilians, Owen's and Queen's Indian setups, and almost every isolated queen's pawn game results in a position with a white pawn on d4 vs. black pawns on e6 and f7.

Black often plays ...h7-h6 of his own accord, after which he might have to close the b1-h7 diagonal (which he damaged with ...h7-h6) with ...g7-g6.

Game 42

Birmingham 1919
White: J.R. Capablanca
Black: T. Bray
Colle System

1.	d4	d5
2.	♘f3	♘f6
3.	e3	e6
4.	♗d3	...

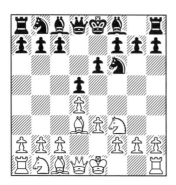

At some point, every chessplayer goes in search of an opening that:

1) is easy to learn;
2) affords attacking chances;
3) entails no material risk.

It's that third requirement that crushes the enterprise in so many players, but I have never understood why. In real life, I can see the desire for low risk, blue-chip investments — people work hard for their money, and count on it being there in case of emergency.

At the chessboard, however, the most speculative ventures can be wildly entertaining, and — at worst — cost nothing but a lost game of chess. The moderate investments — one pawn sacrificed by 1. e4 e5 2. f4 or 1. d4 ♘f6 2. g4 — usually pay dividends in space and mobility, for which the real-life equivalent is vacation.

The Colle System is a low-risk opening that occasionally yields excellent returns in attacking prospects.

| 4. | ... | ♗d6 |

4...♗e7 is more prudent for Black, so when White plays e3-e4, he won't be threatening a pawn fork on e5. Also, if Black feels compelled to swap ...dxe4 (and he usually does), then the recapture ♘xe4 isn't hitting a bishop on d6.

5.	♘bd2	♘bd7
6.	0-0	0-0
7.	♕e2	...

The recipe for this flavor of the Colle is for White to gather his forces behind the e-pawn, and then release the pent-up energy with e3-e4. Black should try to get there first with 7...e5.

| 7. | ... | b6 |

Most of the time, ...b7-b6 can be explained by Black's difficulty in developing his queen's bishop, but right after White plays 7. ♕e2, ...b7-b6 is hard to fathom. Black should know that 8. e4 is coming, and now he can't play 8...dxe4 9. ♘xe4 ♘xe4 10. ♕xe4 ♘f6 because the rook is exposed on a8.

8.	e4	dxe4
9.	♘xe4	♗e7
10.	♖e1	...

Some prefer to play ♖f1-e1 before opening up with e3-e4, but Purdy said that it's usually better to make the pawn advance first. If the rook moves first, and then something happens to make the pawn move inadvisable, then the rook behind the unmoved pawn looks silly.

| 10. | ... | ♖e8 |

If Black could push ...e6-e5, then ...♖f8-e8 is useful, but here it is weakening. 10...♗b7 is sensible.

| 11. | ♘eg5 | ... |

11. ...   ♗b7

Black had to try 11...♞f8 12. ♞e5 ♕xd4.

12. ♞xf7   ♗xf3

Black is smothered by 12...♔xf7 13. ♞g5+ ♔g8 14. ♕xe6+ ♔h8 15. ♞f7+ ♔g8 16. ♞h6+ ♔h8 17. ♕g8+ ♖xg8 18. ♞f7#.

13. gxf3   ♔xf7
14. ♕xe6+   ♔f8
15. ♗c4   1-0

Game 43

New York 1910
White: J.R. Capablanca
Black: Charles Jaffe
Semi-Slav Defense

1. d4   d5
2. ♞f3   ♞f6
3. e3   ...

White has a solid stance in the center, and his kingside development is near completion. There's also a bit of deception built into White's simple sequence: he might continue with c2-c4 to reach a Queen's Gambit, or play either flavor of the Colle System. The only opening White has ruled out

is the Torre Attack 3. ♗g5; even the Stonewall Attack with f2-f4 is possible if White gets around to ♞e5 plus f2-f4.

3. ...   c6
4. c4   e6
5. ♞c3   ♞bd7
6. ♗d3   ...

The most active square for the bishop, while ♗d3 also looks toward White's eventual aim of playing e3-e4. In the 1920s, Black defenders engineered a counter which is still popular: 6...dxc4 7. ♗c4 b5 8. ♗d3 ♗b7 9. 0-0 a6 10. e4 c5.

6. ...   ♗d6

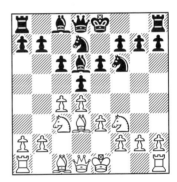

What is good for White at move 6 is not as good for Black. For having the first move, White will achieve e3-e4 before Black can execute ...e6-e5, and because there is a black bishop on d6, a pawn fork will be threatened on e5. Then if Black feels compelled to capture ...dxe4 (and he usually does), White's recapture ♞xe4 will hit the bishop. Black should content himself with 6...♗e7.

7. 0-0   0-0
8. e4   ...

White's central superiority is most evident.

8. ...   dxe4
9. ♘xe4   ♘xe4
10. ♗xe4   ♘f6

Even though Black developed with a threat, he really does not gain a move. The bishop retreats to its desired square, while the f6-knight becomes a target of White's attack. Furthermore, the knight is pulled away from its influence over e5, which makes ...e6-e5 impossible for Black, to the chagrin of his c8-bishop.

In search of an improvement, Black might play to equalize in the center, but 10...e5 loses to 11. dxe5 ♘xe5 12. ♘xe5 ♗xe5 13. ♕h5, so 10...c5 is most preferable.

11. ♗c2   h6

Black fretted over ♕d3 plus ♗g5, ♗xf6, ♕xh7#, but ...h7-h6 just prompts White to aim at the knight from a different diagonal.

12. b3   b6
13. ♗b2   ♗b7

The minor pieces are nearly symmetrical, but the potential for White's pieces is so much greater that the position is nearly a strategic win. White's knight can be posted ideally on e5, whereas Black's knight can't touch e4. White's c2-bishop is ready to form a checkmating battery along the diagonal, while Black's d6-bishop has no such coordination. The queen's bishops are the key to the position: Both bishops require another pawn move to be liberated, but while White's d4-d5 advance will threaten ♗xf6 — winning the game — Black's ...c6-c5 is relatively meaningless.

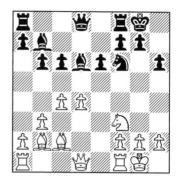

14. ♕d3   g6

14...♖e8 maintains the integrity of the castled wall while giving the king a flight square.

15. ♖ae1   ...

Bringing up new force with the threat ♖xe6!.

15. ...   ♘h5

Black hopes for 16. ♖xe6 ♘f4, but has no luck, or 16...♘g7 to shore up e6, but has no time.

16. ♗c1   ...

Chessplayers learn to move forward, so attacking moves that move backward are most difficult to find. The bishop has greater scope on c1, makes an immediate threat, and stops ...♘f4. The queen's rook has been moved out of the corner, so ♗b2-c1 does not hinder White's mobilization.

16. ...   ♔g7

17. ☖xe6! ...

Threatens to further dynamite Black's structure with 18. ☖xg6!+.

17. ... ☖f6
18. ☖e5! ...

One of the most pleasing aspects of this game is White's nonchalance about the rook hanging on e6. 18. ☖e5 brings more force to bear on the crucial light squares. 18...☖xe5 19. ☖xe5 leaves White in better shape materially as well as positionally.

18. ... c5
19. ☖xh6+ ☗xh6

White's reply does not change in case of 19...☗g8.

20. ☖xf7+ 1-0

Game 44

Hastings 1919
White: J.R. Capablanca
Black: G. Scott
Semi-Slav Defense

1. d4	d5
2. c4	c6
3. ☖f3	☖f6
4. e3	e6
5. ☖bd2	...

The difference between 5. ☖bd2 and 5. ☖c3 shows when Black plays ...dxc4, and White's ☖xc4 piles up on e5.

5. ...	☖bd7
6. ☗d3	☗d6
7. 0-0	0-0
8. e4	dxe4
9. ☖xe4	☖xe4
10. ☗xe4	☖f6
11. ☗c2	b6
12. ☗d3	h6

13. b3 ☗e7

After ...☗e7, e6 is more stable than it was in Capablanca-Jaffe. However, Golombek notes that 13...☗c7 is better because it is so easy for White to play a rook to the e-file and exploit the queen's position.

14. ☗b2 ☖d8

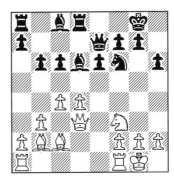

Sturdier than ...g7-g6?, which Jaffe played in the similar position.

15. ☖ad1 ...

Black's care tells on 15. d5 cxd5 16. ☗xf6 ☗xf6 17. ☗h7+ ☗f8 18. cxd5 exd5 19. ☖fe1 ☗e6, which shows that White attacked too soon. Therefore White brings up unused force.

15. ... ☗b7
16. ☖fe1 ☖ac8
17. ☖h4 ...

With ☖f5 in view. The pin on the e6-pawn is why Golombek believed in 13...☗c7.

17. ... ☗b8

Black's reason is that if White plays ☖f5, then it will not be a fork, while Black can answer with ...☗c7 to threaten h2.

18. g3 ...

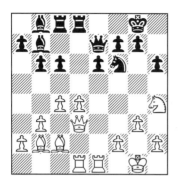

18. ...   ♔f8

Black goes badly adrift. But if he tries to free his b7-bishop and c8-rook with 18...c5, then White pushes forward by 19. d5 e5 20. ♘f5 ♕e8 21. f4, with a winning game.

19. ♕f3   ...

White threatens 20. ♘f5 to split up the black queen and f6-knight, then 21. ♘xh6 gxh6 22. ♕xf6.

19. ...   ♔g8

When a player moves ...♔g8-f8-g8, he is not thinking. If Black were mindful of ♘f5 plus ♘xh6, he would've found 19...♖d7, the only move to keep the queen in touch with f6, so 20. ♘f5 ♕d8 21. ♘xh6 would not be a success.

20. ♘f5   ♕c7
21. ♘xh6+   ♔f8
22. d5   ...

Finally! but only when it makes a genuine threat to f6.

22. ...   cxd5

Suppose Black went back with 22...♕e7 to help the knight, then the 23. ♘f5 trick works a second time: 23...♕e8 24. ♘xg7.

23. ♗xf6   gxf6

If 23...gxh6, then not 24. ♗xd8, but 24. ♕g7 to hunt the king.

24. ♕xf6   ...

The thematic ♖xe6 is back in store, and if 24...♕d7, then 25. ♕h8+ ♔e7 26. ♘f5#.

24. ...   ♔e8
25. ♖xe6+   fxe6
26. ♕xe6+   ♔f8

If 26...♕e7, White brings up new force: 27. ♗g6+ ♔f8 28. ♕g8#.

27. ♕f6+   1-0

27...♔e8 28. ♖e1+ ♕e5 29. ♕f7#.

Game 45

Kolty Chess Club 2007
White: Alexander Levitan
Black: Frisco Del Rosario
Queen's Pawn Game

1. d4   ♘f6
2. ♘f3   d5
3. h3   ...

A tame move that has some explanation. The Russian master likes the London System with 3. ♗f4, but he doesn't like 3...e6 4. e3 ♗d6, when the bishop should move again. He tested 3. h3 against our club fellows, waiting for them to commit their bishops to e7 or d6 before developing his own to f4 or g5. 3. h3 also provides *luft* for the London bishop in event of ...♘h5.

3. ...   c5
4. e3   ♘c6
5. c3   e6
6. ♗d3   ♗d6

Black usually prefers ...♗e7 in such positions, so that the bishop isn't exposed to capture after a pawn exchange brings a white knight forward to c4 or e4, but 3. h3 sort of reversed the colors.

7.	♘bd2	0-0
8.	0-0	e5
9.	dxe5	♘xe5

The d3-bishop was vulnerable to a capture after the pawn trade brought the black knight forward.

10.	♘xe5	♗xe5
11.	♘f3	♗c7
12.	b3	b6
13.	♗b2	♗b7
14.	♕e2	♖e8
15.	♖fd1	♕d6
16.	g3	...

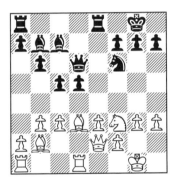

The game has mostly followed Capablanca-Scott, Hastings 1919, in reverse. Capablanca played ♘h4-f5, but Black is a move behind that maneuver, while f4 is under White's control. White's pawn structure suggests that Black play as in Capablanca-Jaffe, Game 43.

16.	...	♘e4
17.	♗xe4	♖xe4
18.	♘g5	♖e5
19.	♕h5	...

White wins the f7-pawn, but Black can plan for ...♖f8 with strong effect.

19.	...	h6
20.	♕xf7+	♔h8

21.	♘f3	...

21...♖f8 would be a mistake: 22. ♘xe5 ♖xf7 23. ♘xf7+.

21.	...	♖xe3!
22.	♘h4	...

Black wins after 22. ♖e1 ♖f8 23. ♕xf8+ ♕xf8 24. ♖xe3 d4, or 22. fxe3 ♕xg3+ 23. ♔f1 d4.

22.	...	♖xg3+!
23.	fxg3	...

If 23. ♘g2, then 23...♖xh3. Or if 23. ♔f1, then 23...♖f8.

23.	...	♕xg3+
24.	♘g2	...

Black wins after 24. ♔f1 d4 25. ♖d2 dxc3 26. ♗xc3 ♗a6+ 27. ♖e2 ♕xc3.

24.	...	d4
25.	♖d2	...

Or 25. ♕f2 ♕h2+ 26. ♔f1 ♗xg2+ 27. ♕xg2 ♖f8+.

25.	...	♕h2+
26.	♔f1	♕h1+
27.	♔e2	♕xg2+
28.	♔e1	♗g3+
29.	♔d1	♗f3+
30.	♔c2	♗e4+

31. ♔c1   ♕g1+
32. ♖d1   ♕e3+
33. ♖d2   ♗e1
0-1

One possibility is 34. ♕f2 ♗xf2 35. cxd4 ♕e1+ 36. ♖d1 ♗e3#. The point to this game is that Black did little original thinking. When chessplayers are steaming from the ears and pulling their hair out at the board, it's because they're working too hard at re-inventing the wheel. By learning good examples at home, much work at the board is already done.

Chapter 14

Mate no. 9

The basis for Mate no. 9 is simple. A bishop on f3/f6 — or anywhere along the long diagonal — combined with rook or queen on the h-file makes checkmates at h1/h8.

Game 46

USSR 1969
White: Konstantin Chernyshov
Black: Andrzej Lesiak
Sokolsky Opening

1. b4 ...

Known as the Polish Opening or the Sokolsky Opening, though one disdainful sort dubbed it the "B-Player Opening" after recognizing 1. b4 as a favorite of local club players.

1. ... e6

The full-blooded 1...e5 2. ♗b2 ♗xb4 3. ♗xe5 ♘f6 plus 4...♘c6 is a test of White's opening, tactically and spiritually: if Black can well afford to trade his e-pawn for the b-pawn, then 1. b4 is for the trash.

2. ♗b2 ♘f6
3. a3 ♗e7

Better is 3...d5 4. e3 c5, filling up the center with a threatening move.

4. e3 0-0
5. ♗d3 h6?

Chess teacher Dan Heisman's "Guide to P-R3" is an instructive article about time wasted and positions ruined by needlessly pushing the a- or h-pawns forward one square. Since the theme of this book is playing for mate, it follows that the losers made too many pawn moves in front of their kings.

6. ♘f3 b6
7. g4 ♗b7
8. g5 hxg5

White is ahead after 8...♘e8 9. gxh6.

9. ♘xg5 ♗xh1?

The best move could be 9...♗d6 with the idea 10. ♗xf6 ♕xf6 11. ♕h5 ♕h6.

10. ♗xf6 g6
11. ♕h5 1-0

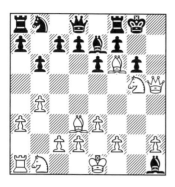

There are three checkmates in store. 11...♗xf6 12. ♕h7# is so commonplace that it isn't categorized in *The Art of the Checkmate*. 11...♖e8 12. ♕h8# is Mate no. 9. 11...gxh5 12. ♗h7# is Blackburne's Mate, the first show of which was N.N.-J.H. Blackburne, London 1880: 1. e4 e5 2. ♘f3 ♘c6 3. ♗c4 ♗c5 4. ♗xf7+ ♔xf7 5. ♘xe5+ ♘xe5 6. ♕h5+ g6 7. ♕xe5 d6 8. ♕xh8 ♕h4 9. 0-0 ♘f6 10. c3 ♘g4 11. h3 ♗xf2+ 12. ♔h1 ♗f5 13. ♕xa8 ♕xh3+ 14. gxh3 ♗xe4#.

Game 47

New York 1918
White: J.R. Capablanca
Black: Frank Marshall
Ruy López

1.	e4	e5
2.	♘f3	♘c6

Capablanca won four games in the 1909 match against Marshall with the Ruy López, after which the American champion switched to Petroff's Defense 2...♘f6. Marshall stuck to the Petroff in five more games (and tried the French Defense once) between 1910 and 1915 before returning to 2...♘c6 at New York 1918. "My first surprise," said Capablanca.

The legend is that Marshall kept his sacrifice at move 8 a secret for years until unveiling it in this game, but in fact Marshall tinkered with it against Frere in 1917, said Chernev in *1000 Best Short Games of Chess*. In Marshall's 1932 book *Comparative Chess*, he didn't give a date for the game against Frere, saying only "the following game was played some years ago to test my new defense in the Ruy López".

Even without fictionalized drama, Capablanca-Marshall, New York 1918, is one of the outstanding games in Capablanca's career, a defensive gem against an eager and well-prepared opponent, while New York 1918 was his best tournament performance ever, according to chessmetrics.com.

3.	♗b5	...

Developing with a threat to threaten. The two-move sequence ♗xc6 plus ♘xe5 will be a real threat after White secures the e4-pawn.

3.	...	a6

White must decide between 4. ♗xc6 — perhaps earlier than he'd like to exchange bishop for lesser minor — or 4. ♗a4, after which Black could end the pressure on the a4-e8 diagonal with ...b7-b5.

4.	♗a4	♘f6
5.	0-0	♗e7

The Open Spanish — 5...♘xe4 6. d4 b5 7. ♗b3 d5 8. dxe5 ♗e6 — is a choice of many who like open games. Marshall played the Open Spanish once, a draw against Leonhardt in Prague 1908, and then came his gambit in the Closed Spanish (which the German master Walbrodt played in Havana 1893, but with far less recognition by chess history).

6. ♖e1	b5
7. ♗b3	0-0

The usual move was 7...d6. Today when a proficient or booked Black plays 7...0-0, White can be sure Marshall's gambit is in store.

8. c3	d5

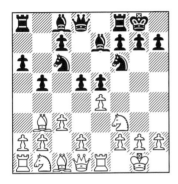

"Now I was sure I had fallen into a prepared variation" — Capablanca.

9. exd5	♘xd5
10. ♘xe5	...

"I [knew] that I would be subjected ... to a terrific attack, whose lines ... would be familiar to my opponent. ... However, my knowledge and judgment told me that my position would be defensible if I accepted the pawn sacrifice. I decided that I was honorbound ... to take the pawn and accept the challenge."

10. ...	♘xe5

One of Black's first points is that White has to exchange a kingside defender in order to accept the gambit.

11. ♖xe5	...

The rook is exposed briefly. 11...c6 to guard the knight, then ...♗e7-d6 to skewer the rook and the h2-pawn is now the preferred move order.

11. ...	♘f6
12. ♖e1	...

The most natural move for controlling the center and starting the queenside development is 12. d4, but Capablanca said he knew the same position would be reached anyway, while 12. ♖e1 might have caused Marshall to benefit less from his homework. "It did not, however, produce such an effect," he wrote.

12. ...	♗d6

Black's pieces are aimed at the denuded white kingside — 13...♘g4 plus 14...♕h4 would start a winning attack — while the white queenside pieces are untouched and the b3-bishop is on the wrong side of the board. These days Marshall's gambit is analyzed past move 30 to an equal game. Its soundness is so well proven that grandmasters who play the Ruy López as White avoid the Marshall if they need a win.

13. h3	♘g4

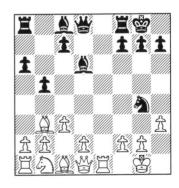

14. ♕f3	...

To be a great defensive player, be a great attacking player first so you can see the tricks coming. Mate no. 9 could follow 14. hxg4 ♕h4 15. ♕f3 ♗h2+ 16. ♔f1 ♗xg4 17. ♕e4 ♗f4! 18. g3 ♕h2! 19. ♖e3 ♖ae8 20. ♕d5 ♗xg3 21. ♖xg3 ♗e2+

22. ♔e1 ♗f3+. Knowing the checkmating patterns contributes to wins, and avoids losses.

14. ...   ♕h4

Ignoring the threat 15. ♕xa8 because Black mates in two after 15... ♕xf2+.

15. d4   ...

Whether White plays this at move 12 or 15, he can't survive Black's attack unless he mobilizes his idle queenside.

15. ...   ♘xf2

Capablanca's notes in the tournament book said, "Very likely a mistake and overlooking the reply. 15...h5 was perhaps the best way to keep up the pressure." Introducing new force with 15...h5 enables Black to bring the bishop forward with ...♗g4 in case of hxg4.

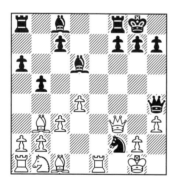

16. ♖e2   ...

"The trapper trapped," Capablanca wrote in *My Chess Career*, adding that Black gets a winning attack after 16. ♕xf2 ♗h2+ (16. ... ♗g3? enables the elementary back-rank trick 17. ♕xf7+ ♖xf7 18. ♖e8#) 17. ♔f1 ♗g3 18. ♕e2 ♗xh3 19. gxh3 ♖ae8.

16. ...   ♗g4

Black also has to use inactive force. Khalifman's crew says White wins after 16...♘g4? 17. g3 ♕xh3 18. ♕xa8 ♕xg3+ 19. ♕g2 ♕h4 20. ♘d2 ♗h2+ 21. ♔f1.

17. hxg4   ♗h2+
18. ♔f1   ♗g3
19. ♖xf2   ...

White almost has the game turned around, considering the material imbalance and center control, while he has more pieces working than Black does. Black can't threaten mate by 19...♖ae8 because White replies 20. ♗xf7+.

19. ...   ♕h1+
20. ♔e2   ♗xf2

Black is grabbing inactive pieces with 20...♕xc1 21. ♕xg3 ♕xb2+ 22. ♘d2 ♕xa1, and suddenly White has activity and initiative following 23. ♖xf7.

21. ♗d2!   ...

A smart little move. Capturing on f2 allows 21...♕xc1 with a threat to b2, so White instead develops his threatened piece with a threat to capture. Threats are more powerful than their execution.

21. ...   ♗h4
22. ♕h3   ♖ae8+
23. ♔d3   ♕f1+
24. ♔c2   ♗f2
25. ♕f3   ...

The pin on the f2-bishop inhibits Black's coordination by ...♖e8-e2 plus ...♗f2-e3, while White's pieces cooperate to tie the f8-rook to the defense of f7.

25. ...   ♕g1
26. ♗d5!   ...

To activate his queenside pieces, White must break the pin on his knight. One way would be to move the rook off the first rank, but first White has to get the pawn out of the way by a2-a4xb5. If White plays a2-a4 too soon, Black can keep the file closed with ...b5-b4, so White aims to fix the b5-pawn with b2-b4, before which he has to move his bishop.

26. ...   c5
27. dxc5   ♗xc5

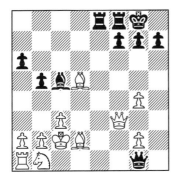

28. b4   ♗d6

28. ... ♗e3 29. ♗xe3 ♖xe3 30. ♘d2! — Capablanca.

29. a4   a5
30. axb5   axb4
31. ♖a6   ...

Whether at move 3 or move 31, you should develop with threats.

31. ...   bxc3
32. ♘xc3   ♗b4
33. b6   ...

His development finally complete, White can play an ending by pushing his passed pawn.

33. ...   ♗xc3
34. ♗xc3   h6
35. b7   ♖e3
36. ♗xf7+   1-0

Chapter 15

Pillsbury's Mate

Most successful attacks against a castled king require a breach in the castled position, often by means of a sacrifice. For instance, Greco's classical bishop sacrifice, Lasker's double bishop sacrifice, and Anastasia's checkmating pattern hinge around a piece gambited on KR7.

Pillsbury's and Morphy's mates are closely related, cracking the enemy king position by opening the g-file with the offer of a piece.

Pillsbury's Mate

1.	♖xg7+	♔h8
2.	♖g8+	♔xg8
3.	♖g1#	1-0

Morphy's Mate

1.	♕xf6	gxf6
2.	♖g1+	♔h8
3.	♗xf6#	

Game 48

Berlin 1928
White: Richard Réti
Black: J.R. Capablanca
Ruy López

1.	e4	...

From 1917 to 1924, Capablanca did not lose a single tournament game, an undefeated stretch so long that it helped form Capablanca's reputation as "the chess machine." But at

New York 1924, the Czech grandmaster Réti beat Capablanca to end the streak. Berlin 1928 was their next encounter.

1.	...	e5
2.	♘f3	♘c6
3.	♗b5	d6

An old master said that Capablanca played the Steinitz Defense when he was "young and hungry." Capablanca preferred the flexible 3...a6 4. ♗a4 ♘f6 5. 0-0 ♗e7 as early as 1913. Playing 3...d6 against Réti suggests that perhaps Capablanca had a chip on his shoulder.

4.	c3	a6
5.	♗a4	f5

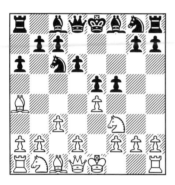

Compare the Siesta Variation to other Black counterattacks with an early ...f7-f5. The Latvian Gambit 1. e4 e5 2. ♘f3 f5 3. ♘xe5 enables the knight to capture in the center. Philidor improved the move order with 1. e4 e5 2. ♘f3 d6 3. d4 f5, when the knight can't centralize with 4. ♘xe5, but 4. ♗c4 prevents kingside castling, while 4. ♘c3 readies for 4...fxe4 5. ♘xe4 with good development.

Schliemann's defense to the Ruy López — 1. e4 e5 2. ♘f3 ♘c6 3. ♗b5 f5 — is also well met by 4. ♘c3. The Siesta move order holds ...f5 back until White has blocked his knight from c3.

6.	d4	...

6. exf5 is recommended in theory so that Black cannot play ...fxe4 as a threatening move.

6.	...	fxe4
7.	♘g5	exd4

Black played woefully in Bruckhaus-Schack, Barmen 1935: 7...b5 8. ♗b3 d5 9. dxe5 ♘ce7 10. 0-0 h6 11. ♘xe4 dxe4 12. ♗f7+ 1-0.

8.	♘xe4	♘f6

Suetin played 8...♗f5, but it's a position for developing knights before bishops. Black can't be sure ...♗f5 is the correct bishop development, while ...♘f6 is the only knight development that threatens.

9.	♗g5	♗e7

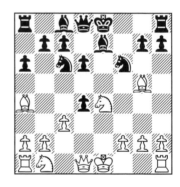

10.	♕xd4?	...

The move leading to White's defeat. In E. Steiner-Kmoch, Budapest 1928, White attacked with his queen rather than let her be attacked: 10. ♗xf6 ♗xf6 11. ♕h5+ g6 12. ♕d5.

10.	...	b5

The unpinning move creates two threats.

11. ♞xf6+   gxf6

Three white pieces are in danger. 11...♝xf6 12. ♝xf6 would have let White off the hook.

12. ♛d5   bxa4
13. ♝h6   ...

13. ♛xc6+ ♝d7 14. ♛f3 fxg5 15. ♛h5+ ♚f8 should be an easy win for Black, a piece ahead and with better development.

13. ...   ♛d7
14. 0-0   ♝b7
15. ♝g7   0-0-0!

By ignoring the threat, Black is enabled to coordinate an attack against the white king.

16. ♝xh8   ♞e5

Remarkably, the white queen in the center of the board has just two safe places to run: a5 and d1. 16. ♛d4 and 16. ♛d2 both lose to 16...♞f3+.

17. ♛d1   ♝f3!
18. gxf3   ...

Otherwise 18...♛g4 with mate to follow.

18. ...   ♛h3
19. ♚h1   ♞xf3
20. ♛xf3   ♛xf3+
21. ♚g1   ♜g8+
0-1

Game 49

La Habana 1902
White: Juan Corzo
Black: J.R. Capablanca
French Defense

1. e4   e6

Purdy considered 1...e6 Black's second-best reply to 1. e4. Black frees the same pieces, and even makes the first threat with 2. d4 d5. Then if White plays 3. ♞c3, Black can renew the threat with 3...♞f6, and then if 4. ♝g5, Black can renew for a second time with 4...♝b4. Should White feel pressured into advancing to e5, the white pawn center is fixed and can be attacked with ...c7-c5 and/or ...f7-f6. The drawbacks to the French Defense are a space disadvantage for Black and a bad queen's bishop.

2. d4   d5
3. ♞c3   dxe4

As a mature master, Capablanca preferred the 3...♞f6 4. ♝g5 ♝b4 development.

4. ♞xe4   ♝d7

4...♞f6 is the development that immediately threatens the white knight, but 4...♝d7 includes the positional logic that Black is moving his bad bishop from behind the e6-pawn. 4...♝d7 appealed to Karpov, the modern world champion stylistically closest to Capablanca. 4...b6 is not as solid; in Tal-Kholmov, Moscow 1975, White pounced on the diagonal with 5. ♛f3.

5. ♞f3   ♝c6
6. ♝d3   ♞d7
7. 0-0   ♞gf6
8. ♝g5   ...

A natural move, but 8. ♞g3 is preferable. Black would like to ease his cramped position with exchanges — when Black unpins, the threat to capture on e4 is renewed, while the bishop on g5 is exposed to threats both discovered and direct.

8. ...   ♝e7

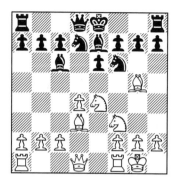

9. ♘xf6+ ...

Materially-equal exchanges favor the side whose pieces come forward as a result of the swap. 9. ♘xf6+ brings a black piece forward, where it makes a threat. If White plays 9. ♘g3, Black can discover with ...♘d5, while 9...0-0 10. c4 ♗xf3 11. ♕f3 c5 12. ♗e3 abashed the bishop into losing a move in Perényi-Dobosz, Szolnok 1985.

9. ... ♗xf6

10. ♗e3 ...

10. ♗xf6 compounds the problem: 10...♕xf6 is a gain of time, and threatens to break up White's structure with 11...♗xf3.

10. ... 0-0
11. c3 b6

Now that Black has developed, it is wise to play ...b7-b6, giving the bishop a retreat in case of ♘e5, while the b6-pawn can help Black hit the center with ...c5.

12. ♕c2 ♔h8

The players agreed in the assessment that 12...♗xf3 13. gxf3 favors White, considering his better center control and development. Most would move the target with 12...h6, but the young player made the more impudent move.

13. ♘d2 ...

White couldn't grab the h7-pawn right away: 13. ♗xh7 ♗xf3 14. gxf3 g6 15. ♗xg6 fxg6 16. ♕xg6 ♖g8.

13. ... ♖e8

Black is playing cat-and-mouse.

14. ♗xh7 g6
15. ♗xg6 fxg6
16. ♕xg6 ♕e7

Three pawns is insufficient for the piece when the side with the piece is better developed, and on the verge of seizing the initiative. White should interfere with Black's coordination against g2 with 17. ♘e4 ♖g8 18. ♕h6+ ♕h7 19. ♕xh7+ ♔xh7 20. ♘xf6+ ♗xf6 21. f3.

17. f4 ♕h7
18. ♕xh7+ ...

A retreat along the g-file loses more time to 18...♖g8.

18. ... ♔xh7
19. ♘f3 ♖g8
20. ♖ae1 ♖g6

The most sensible rook lift. ♘either 20...♖g7 nor 20...♖g4 enables Black to shift the rook to the h-file if desired.

21. ♗d2 ♗d5
22. b3 ♖f8

White would be alert after 22...♖ag8, but the modest 22...♖f8 might encourage White to play 23. c4 ♗xf3 24. ♖xf3 ♗xd4+.

23. ♔h1 c5

Introducing the most available new force with a threat: ...♗xf3 plus ...cxd4.

24. dxc5   ...

Another swap that loses time. 24. ♗e3 is a wretched move, but White is spellbound into keeping the line open to the e6-pawn, and driving off the defender with c3-c4.

24. ...   ♘xc5

Black's knight came forward purposefully: to threaten the win of at least a pawn with 25...♘e4, and to put another guard on e6.

25. c4   ♗a8
26. ♗b4   ...

White chased one protector away; now he works on the other.

26. ...   ♖fg8
27. ♗xc5   ...

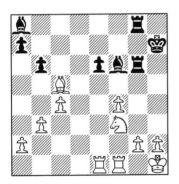

27. ...   ♖xg2!

Before White can close the file with 28. g3.

28. ♗e3   ...

Moving on the a3-f8 diagonal runs into mate: 28...♖g1+ 29. ♖xg1 ♗xf3+ 30. ♖g2 ♗xg2+ 31. ♔g1 ♗d4+. Ironically, e3 — a square on which the bishop blocks the rook's sight of e6 — is the only reasonable square. 28. ♗f2 ♗xf3 loses, and so do 28. ♗d4 ♗xd4 29. ♘xd4 ♖g1# and 28. ♗g1 ♖xg1+!.

28. ...   ♗h4
29. ♖d1   ♗f2

Black menaces 30...♖g1+ 31. ♖xg1 ♗xf3+ 32. ♖g2 ♗xg2#.

30. ♖d7+   ...

The bishop is immune: 30. ♖xf2 ♖xf2 and 30. ♗xf2 ♗xf3 both lose.

30. ...   ♔h6
31. ♖d5   ♗xe3
32. ♘g5   ...

31. ♖d5 and 32. ♘g5 have the same feel as spite checks, which delay losses but don't prevent them.

32. ...   ♖2xg5
33. fxg5+   ♖xg5
34. ♖f6+   ♔h5
35. ♖xe6   ...

White's mission is complete, but Tartakover said there are no moral victories in chess.

35. ...   ♗xd5+
36. cxd5   ♖g1#
0-1

Chapter 16

Mates with Major Pieces

After a student learns how the pieces move, and gets some grasp of the concept of checkmate, the "rook roller" is often his first lesson in coordinating the pieces. "The first thing a student should do," said Capablanca, "is to familiarize himself with the power of the pieces. This can best be done by learning how to accomplish quickly some of the simple mates."

1. &h5 ...

In any endgame with rooks, the rook's first job is to threaten things. Its second job is to take things, because that frees the rook to attack other things. The rook's third job is to cut off mobility.

In the rook roller pattern, the defending king's mobility is cut off row by row until mate is delivered. Neither 1. &h6+ nor 1. &c4+ drives the black king toward the edge of the board. Other logical cutting-off moves are 1. &d2 and 1. &g5.

1. ... &d6
2. &g6+ ...

The rooks cooperate by squeezing one row of life per turn from the black king. 2. &e4 is not quite as accurate, because it doesn't immediately remove a row of space: 2...&c6 3. &e6+ &d7 4. &g6 &e7 5. &h7+ &f8 6. &g1 &e8 7. &g8#.

2. ... &e7
3. &h7+ &f8
4. &a6 ...

Another thing to learn in this endgame is that 4. &g8+ would be a slip, so the rook swings to other side of the board in order to threaten mate. In the interest of efficiency, the best move is 5. &g1 (5...&e8 6. &g8#), though chess teachers can find that teaching the correct maneuver adds another layer of abstraction.

4. ... &g8
5. &b7 ...

Now 5. &a8+ is the mixup, so the h7-rook also slides away. A little subtlety is that it should not move to the a-file, where the rooks get in each other's way.

5. ... &h8
6. &a8# 1-0

I didn't learn this queen-and-rook pattern until I was an old dog rated 2100. If one doesn't learn it, the finish to Capablanca-Chajes is harder to find.

1.	☐c5+	♔d6
2.	♕c7+	♔e6
3.	☐e5+	♔f6
4.	♕e7+	♔g6
5.	☐g5+	♔h6
6.	♕g7#	1-0

1. ♕c5+ ♔d7 2. ♕b6 ♔e7 3. ☐a7+ ♔e8 4. ♕b8# and 1. ♕d4 ♔c7 2. ☐c5+ ♔b6 3. ♕b4+ ♔a6 4. ☐a5# are shorter wins, but that isn't the idea of the diagram. Extra credit for 1. ♕e7 ♔b6 2. ☐c5 ♔a6 3. ♕h7! ♔b6 4. ♕c7+ ♔a6 5. ☐a5#, which saves a move while sticking to the lesson plan.

Game 50

New York 1913
White: J.R. Capablanca
Black: Oscar Chajes
Ruy López

1.	e4	e5
2.	♘f3	♘c6
3.	♗b5	...

A most general formula for winning a chess game: Get better center control, better development, and better king safety. Then from that superior position — with better center control, development, and king safety, your position is superior — attack the enemy king, usually by opening files

for your major pieces.

The Ruy López follows the recipe more closely than other open games. The center pawns are equal, but White has a long-term threat to win the center and material by capturing first on c6, then e5. He is ahead in development, and is two moves closer to castling than Black.

3.	...	a6

When Black plays 3...a6, he queries the bishop: "Would you care to exchange yourself for a lesser minor piece now, or would you prefer to drop back to a4, after which I might play ... b7-b5 to relieve the pressure on the a4-e8 diagonal (though I am aware that ...b7-b5 weakens my queenside pawns)?"

4.	♗a4	♘f6

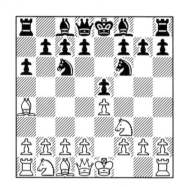

5.	0-0	...

Ignoring the threat to e4. 5. d3, 5. ♕e2, and 5. ♘c3 are O.K., but more committal.

5.	...	b5

In the Open Variation, Black carries out his threat: 5...♘xe4 6. d4 b5 7. ♗b3 d5 8. dxe5 ♗e6. It's not as popular as 5...♗e7 because while Black has mobile pieces, the pawn position is unexciting.

6.	&b3	&e7
7.	d4	...

Ignoring the hit to e4. If 7...♘xe4, then 8. dxe5 threatens 9. &xf7+, so 8...0-0 9. &d5 ♘c5, when White has an option to head for a winning ending with &xc6.

7.	...	d6
8.	c3	...

In order to replace the d4-pawn with another pawn, and with an air of nonchalance. If 8...♘xe4, then 9. &d5 forks.

8.	...	&g4

Threatens ...&xf3, when White must either gambit the d-pawn with ♕xf3 or fracture his castled position.

9.	&e3	0-0
10.	♘bd2	♘a5
11.	&c2	♖e8
12.	b4	...

White can gain bishop for knight by 12. dxe5 dxe5 13. h3, but that would give up his central superiority.

12.	...	exd4

Black thought to give up the center so that his knight retreat would threaten b4, and afford him the time to rearrange his pieces. Black didn't like the looks of 12...♘c6 13. d5 or 12...♘c4 13. ♘xc4 bxc4, where the c-pawn is a target following 14. dxe5 dxe5 15. ♕xd8 &xd8 16. ♘d2.

13.	cxd4	♘c6
14.	a3	&f8

If 15. d5, then the knight has a central retreat, but for the opening of the c-file, White can menace the knight.

15.	♖c1	♘e7
16.	e5!	...

If the knight is driven away, White discovers a threat on the g4-bishop with &xh7+ plus ♘g5+.

16.	...	dxe5

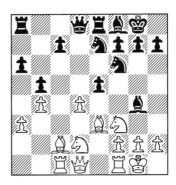

17.	dxe5	&xf3

Preventing the combination but losing time because White's pieces develop with the recapture.

18.	♕xf3	♘d7
19.	♕h3	...

Not only can 19. ♕h5 be met by 19...g6, 19. ♕h3 is stronger because the queen presses on the d7-knight, making threats possible.

19.	...	♘g6
20.	f4	♘b6
21.	♘f3	♘c4

On 21...h6, White continues strongly with 22. ♖fd1 ♕b8 23. &b3 to pin f7, so that 24. ♖c6 or 24. ♕f5 threatens the g6-knight.

22.	♘g5	h6
23.	♘xf7	♔xf7
24.	♕f5+	♔g8
25.	♕xg6	...

White must have been aware that the e3-bishop would be hanging at the end, but it's relatively without value as it's not contributing to the attack.

25. ...	♞xe3
26. ♕h7+	♔f7
27. ♗b3+	♞c4
28. ♖fd1!	...

Every white piece is working, while Black is prevented from mobilizing his queen with ...♕d8-d4+. It's the kind of move that separates good players from bad players.

28. ...	♕b8
29. ♖xc4!	bxc4
30. ♗xc4+	♔e7
31. ♕f5	...

Threatening three checkmates.

31. ...	♕b6+
32. ♔f1	1-0

When Capablanca sat down to write *Chess Fundamentals*, he asked: "What's the first position the student should see?" The greatest natural chessplayer ever thought that the first thing the student should learn is how to mate with king and rook:

1. ♖a7	...

The first priority for a rook in a rook ending is to threaten stuff. The second priority is to take stuff. The third is to cut off the enemy's mobility.

In this position with nothing to threaten and nothing to capture, the rook cuts off. "The principle," according to *Chess Fundamentals* "is to drive the opposing king to the last line on any side of the board."

1. ...	♔g8
2. ♔g2	...

"Keep [the] king as much as possible on the same rank or file as the opposing king."

2. ...	♔f8
3. ♔f3	♔e8
4. ♔e4	♔d8
5. ♔d5	♔c8
6. ♔d6!	♔b8
7. ♖c7	♔a8
8. ♔c6	♔b8
9. ♔b6	♔a8
10. ♖c8#	1-0

The old cliché is, "It's what you learn after you know it all that matters." I didn't learn the queen-plus-rook pattern described before Capablanca-Chajes until I'd been an expert for 10 years. Same goes for this pattern with lone rook:

1. ♖h5	

The key first move is "any rook move," like 1. ♖a1 (except for 1. ♖g1?, any rook move will do, as long as White's second move cuts off the black king) ♔g8 2. ♖f1 ♔h8 3. ♖f8#.

The queen-plus-rook and "any rook move" patterns were holes in my knowledge after 30 years of tournament play! Tal read a beginners' book every year because the world champion knew there's always some patch to acquire for a crack in one's chess foundation.

1. ...   ♔g8
2. ♖f5   ♔h8
3. ♖f8#   1-0

Game 51

New York 1924
White: J.R. Capablanca
Black: Savielly Tartakover
Dutch Defense

1. d4   ...

One of the grand descriptions of chess is "a battle of time, force, and space." In discussions of time at chess, we talk about time units of a single move ("a tempo"), but each of those individual steps is part of a longer event. There is the sprint toward full piece mobility, then the late kick to get to the other side of the board.

Sometimes the race to the other side is short, when one side builds a mating attack, but sometimes the race is a marathon, where the winning side promotes a pawn one step ahead of the other. In the opening phase, a gambit is a common investment of material for a gain of time, but as the game progresses, material sacrifices grow less frequent and more dramatic.

Capablanca-Tartakover, New York 1924, is a landmark example of material sacrifice in the late game for the sake of mobility and time.

1. ...   f5

1...f5 doesn't aid in Black's development and weakens his king position, but it hits the center and unbalances the position. A chess game is long enough that one flawed move in the opening — unless it is a tactical blunder — is a blink in time. The importance of each move is magnified in the endgame, when one imperfect move can turn a win into a loss.

2. ♘f3   ...

Capablanca recommended Staunton's gambit 2. e4, but against very good opposition, he was circumspect.

2. ...   e6

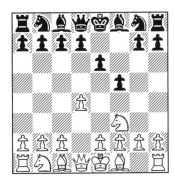

3. c4   ...

3. e4 can also be played now: former world champion Smyslov lost to 3...fxe4 4. ♘g5 in 1995.

3. ...   ♘f6
4. ♗g5   ...

The pivotal square is e4. Black played to control it, then White pinned the f6-knight in contest. White could have played his pawn to e4 on move 2 when it was enterprising, on move 3 when it was novel, or he might achieve the e4 advance when it is entirely sound.

4.	...	♗e7
5.	♘c3	0-0
6.	e3	...

Experience shows that a kingside fianchetto is good against the Dutch. From g2, the bishop watches the critical e4 square from a greater distance, so in case of exchanges on e4, a black pawn landing there won't bother the bishop.

| 6. | ... | b6 |

The queen's bishop is a problem piece for Black in most queen's pawn openings, especially the Dutch (in the Stonewall Variation, Black puts two more pawns on d5 and c6 to block that poor bishop). 6...b6 plus ...♗b7 will develop the bishop outside the d7-e6-f5 pawn chain, and aim at e4, but if a fight breaks out on the kingside, a bishop on b7 might be unable to participate.

Also, if White develops his bishop on g2, there's the potential for a tactical trick: when White's kingside fianchettoed bishop collides with Black's queenside fianchettoed bishop, the g2-bishop is usually guarded by a castled king, but the b7-bishop is often hanging. Since White signaled a different bishop development when he played e2-e3, that trick is less likely.

| 7. | ♗d3 | ♗b7 |
| 8. | 0-0 | ♕e8 |

A typical queen move in Dutch positions. The queen might improve on g6 or h5, or aid a pawn's advance to e5.

| 9. | ♕e2 | ♘e4 |

A panicky play, especially in relation to his previous move.

| 10. | ♗xe7 | ... |

If Black hadn't played 8...♕e8, then he would have gained a move here.

| 10. | ... | ♘xc3 |
| 11. | bxc3 | ♕xe7 |

| 12. | a4 | ... |

Logical. Perhaps White will get rid of his weakest pawn and gain scope for his queen's rook, while Black is deprived of ...♕a3 as a threatening move.

| 12. | ... | ♗xf3 |

A puzzling decision, giving up bishop for knight while lessening his influence over e4, the square he's been fighting for since move one. 12...♘c6 plus ...♘a5, ...c7-c5, and ...♗b7-a6 would be a typical scheme to blockade and attack the c-pawns.

| 13. | ♕xf3 | ♘c6 |
| 14. | ♖fb1 | ♖ae8 |

Black plans ...e6-e5, but White shuts that down neatly.

| 15. | ♕h3! | ... |

White's queen move inhibits 15...e5, which would lose the f5-pawn. 15. ♕h3 also freed the f-pawn so that it could help control e5.

15. ...	♖f6
16. f4	♘a5
17. ♕f3	...

The queen now supports White's own e-pawn advance.

17. ...	d6
18. ♖e1	♕d7
19. e4	fxe4
20. ♕xe4	g6

Creates an object for White's attack, but after 20...♖h6, the rook is tied to the defense of h7, and Black might end up playing ...g7-g6 anyway.

21. g3	...

The first step in a plan to attack g6.

21. ...	♔f8
22. ♔g2	♖f7
23. h4	d5

Results in an inferior endgame, but White was heading for a strong initiative with 24. h5. White's attack on the h-file would've also followed 23...♘xc4 24. ♗xc4 d5 25. ♗xd5 (the trouble with 25. ♕e5 dxc4 is that Black threatens ...♕d5+) 25...exd5 26. ♕xe8+ ♕xe8 27. ♖xe8+ ♔xe8 28. h5.

24. cxd5	exd5
25. ♕xe8+	♕xe8
26. ♖xe8+	♔xe8

27. h5	...

In advance of ♖e1-h1, and then penetration along the h-file. A chess teacher once said, "Everybody thinks Morphy always played ♖e1+," alluding to his students' guessing the obvious "biggest unused force with a check," even when Morphy played a move that better met the demands of the position. The same reasoning applies to a Capablanca game — White could play 27. ♖e1+, but then 27...♔f8 28. h5 gxh5 and White should play 29. ♖h1.

27. ...	♖f6
28. hxg6	hxg6
29. ♖h1	♔f8
30. ♖h7	♖c6
31. g4	...

Mobilizing the pawn majority, perhaps with 32. g5, 33. ♖h6, and 34. f5 to come.

31. ...	♘c4
32. g5	♘e3+
33. ♔f3	♘f5

34. ♗xf5!	...

Giving up bishop for knight to gain a passed pawn, plus the king's safe passage along the h-file. The risky beauty of this is that White abandons

143

his pawns while activating his king. In the opening, one inactive piece means a slight disadvantage of 8 to 7 in piece activity, but in the ending, one inactive piece means a decisive 2-to-1 deficit. White's king is an active, attacking piece, while Black's king is under fire.

34. ...	gxf5
35. ♔g3	♖xc3+
36. ♔h4	♖f3

Black is a pawn ahead, but he mustn't trade the rooks: 36...♖c1 37. ♔h5 ♖h1+ 38. ♔g6 ♖xh7 39. ♔xh7 wins for White.

37. g6! ...

Ignoring the threat to f4 in order to increase the king's activity.

| 37. ... | ♖xf4+ |
| 38. ♔g5 | ♖e4 |

Black can eat until he explodes: 38...♖xd4 39. ♔f6 ♔g8 40. ♖d7 (how fitting that White should not capture with 40. ♖xc7, enabling the defense 40...♖c4).

39. ♔f6 ...

Threatening mate is much stronger than 39. ♔xf5, which does not threaten, and enables Black to check on the f-file.

39. ...	♔g8
40. ♖g7+	♔h8
41. ♖xc7	...

Alekhine wrote a memorable note hereabouts: "Black's pawns fall like ripe apples."

41. ...	♖e8
42. ♔xf5	♖e4
43. ♔f6	♖f4+
44. ♔e5	♖g4

| 45. g7+ | ♔g8 |

Not 45...♖xg7, because the easiest endings to win are pure pawn endings: 46. ♖xg7 ♔xg7 47. ♔xd5 ♔f7 48. ♔d6 ♔e8 49. ♔c7.

46. ♖xa7	♖g1
47. ♔xd5	♖c1
48. ♔d6	♖c2
49. d5	♖c1
50. ♖c7	♖a1
51. ♔c6	♖xa4
52. d6	1-0

Game 52

New York 1906
White: Robert Raubitschek
Black: J.R. Capablanca
King's Gambit

| 1. e4 | e5 |
| 2. f4 | ... |

Tarrasch said the hardest thing to do at chess is to win a won game, so a chess teacher might encourage his students to give their opponents the problem of having a won game right away.

Most gambits are incorrect. To give up a pawn in the opening for less than three moves in development, deflecting the enemy queen, preventing the opponent from castling, or building up an attack leads — technically speaking — to a lost game. But gambiteers learn to love having to prove their enterprise, while the opponents' practical difficulties of converting a small material gain into a point are great.

2. ...   exf4

2. f4 is a speculative venture. 2. f4 does not truly threaten, because if Black passed and White "carried out" 3. fxe5, then 3...♕h4 wrecks White's position. 2. f4 does not aid White's development. 2. f4 permanently weakens White's kingside.

But if White's deflection of the Black e-pawn results in center control for White with a d2-d4 advance while he gets his pieces out, and if White can then make use of the open f-file, the returns on the initial investment can be spectacular. In the immediate short term, White has zero return on investment — he can't even take the center with 3. d4 because 3...♕h4 lurks.

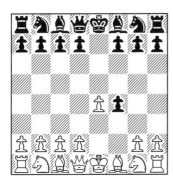

3. ♘f3   ...

A sharper alternative is 3. ♗c4, which better inhibits ...d7-d5, but invites 3...♕h4+ 4. ♔f1. 3. ♘c3 ♕h4+ 4. ♔e2 may be overdoing it, though Keres danced on that wire.

3. ...   g5

The f4-pawn is critical to the position. White hopes to achieve d2-d4 plus ♗xf4, making his positional goal while recovering the material investment. With 3...g5, Black tries to contain the c1-bishop, which in turn blocks the a1-rook. Preserving the material gain is almost an afterthought.

4. ♗c4   ...

4. h4 is a stronger move for the positional logic described earlier. Then Black cannot maintain his restraining pawn structure with 4...h6 because 5. hxg5 shows the h6-pawn to be pinned.

4. ...   ♗g7

Guarding the rook enables ...h7-h6 to support the pawn formation.

5. h4   ...

Too late. The butterfly effect from White's not breaking down the f4-g5 pawn formation with 4. h4 is Black's ability to sacrifice them later.

5. ...   h6

The f4-g5 pawns stand, so White's queenside has greater difficulty mobilizing.

6. d4   ♘c6

Black threatens 7...g4 plus 8...♘xd4. White might not mind so much (because his ♗xf4 development becomes possible again) if his knight had a more useful place to flee to than h2.

7. c3   d6
8. 0-0   ...

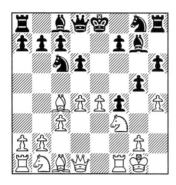

8. ...   ♕e7

8...g4 is a bad idea for Black: 9. ♘e1 ♕xh4 10. ♗xf4, and storm clouds gather on the f-file.

9. ♕b3   ...

Maybe White was pondering 10. hxg5 hxg5 11. ♕b5, hitting g5 while pinning c6 and threatening 12. d5. If he wasn't thinking about it, Black waved a cape in that direction by moving the knight so that ♕b5 will be a check.

9. ...   ♘d8

This game demonstrated that sacrificing the g5-structure held promise. Over the years, the developing move 9...♘f6 emerged as the best way to draw White's attention toward g5. Then 10. hxg5 hxg5 11. ♘xg5 ♘xd4 12. ♗xf7+ ♔d8 13. cxd4 ♘xe4, and Black has a strong attack.

10. hxg5   hxg5
11. ♕b5+   ...

It's easy to understand why White took the bait — when the pawns disappear, his f1-rook and c1-bishop are freed — but Black makes three straight developing moves that attack the queen. White needed to play 4. h4.

11. ...   ♗d7

12. ♕xg5   ♗f6
13. ♕xf4   ♘e6
14. ♗xe6   ♗xe6

15. e5   ...

This advance creates space on e4, so White's pieces must be ready to use the space: 15. ♗e3 0-0-0 16. ♘bd2. Only then e4-e5, with ♘e4 to follow.

15. ...   dxe5
16. ♘xe5   0-0-0
17. ♘a3   ...

The knight is out of play. 17. ♗e3 with ♘d2 still seems indicated.

17. ...   ♖h4
18. ♕g3   ♗xe5

A constructive liquidation, opening g4 for the h4-rook, while the d8-rook improves no matter which way White recaptures.

19. ♕xe5   ♖d5
20. ♕g7   ...

White has to make a threat, else 20...♖dh5 is coming. 20. ♕g3 is better than 20. ♕g7 because 21...♘f6 won't be an attacking move, but White didn't see Black's 22nd.

20. ...   ♖g4
21. ♕h7   ♘f6
22. ♕h8+   ♖d8!

Ignoring two threats enables Black to coordinate the rooks.

23. ♕xf6   ♖dg8!
24. ♖f2   ...

24. ♕xe7 ♖xg2+ 25. ♔h1 ♗d5 threatens 26...♖h8+ and 26...♖f2+.

24. ...   ♖xg2+
25. ♔f1   ♗c4+
26. ♘xc4   ♖g1#
0-1

Game 53

Berlin 1913
White: J.R. Capablanca
Black: Jacques Mieses
Benoni Defense

1. d4   ♘f6
2. ♘f3   c5

The Benoni in its many forms gained popularity in the '60s, when Black embraced the notion of fighting for the initiative immediately instead of working toward equality first. The most sorcerous of world champions, Tal, played the Modern Benoni during the 1960 world championship match, as did Fischer in 1972.

3. d5   ...

The most double-edged move, taking up the center space that Black did not contest. If White is in less of a punishing mood, 3. e3 and 3. c4 are also good.

3. ...   d6
4. c4   g6

It took a few decades for the gambits like 4...b5 5. cxb5 a6 6. bxa6 g6 to gain traction.

5. ♘c3   ♗g7
6. e4   0-0
7. ♗e2   ...

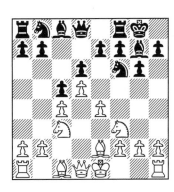

Compare this to a typical King's Indian Defense — 1. d4 ♘f6 2. c4 g6 3. ♘c3 ♗g7 4. e4 d6 5. ♘f3 0-0 6. ♗e2 e5 7. d5 — where Black is closer to being equally placed in the center, and will strive for a kingside initiative with ... f7-f5, while a common plan for White is to play on the queenside with b2-b4 plus c4-c5. In the Benoni, Black plays on the queenside — because he usually has a pawn majority there — while e5 is a desirable square for a knight, and the e-file is open for a black rook.

The trouble with Black's game becomes the backward pawn on d6, which is the only pawn in the way of White's crashing through with f2-f4 plus e4-e5.

7. ...   e6
8. 0-0   exd5
9. exd5   ...

A gentler move than 9. cxd5, which unbalances the center and the queenside. 9. exd5 takes more of the center, but affords Black additional counterplay along the e-file and with his queenside pawn majority. 9. cxd5 is the move you'd play if you were confident in beating your opponent even by cultivating a smaller advantage.

9. ...   ♞e8

Black can't afford to undevelop his pieces while he is already behind in development. Any developing move is better — 9...♖e8 fits in with the idea that it's wise to finish development on one side of the board first.

10. ♖e1   ♝g4
11. ♞g5   ...

A powerful move. If Black swaps on e2, White gains time with the recapture, while the knight on g5 means to circle back to e4 where it hits the weak d6-pawn. (If White had played 9. cxd5, this knight would have maneuvered ♞d2-c4 for the same reason).

11. ...   ♝xc3

Black cripples White's queenside pawns, which become immobile and would be subject to attack if Black weren't so far behind in development. Dzindzichashvili championed this idea in the '80s — with the move order 1.d4 g6 2.c4 ♝g7 3.♞c3 c5 4.d5 ♝xc3 5.bxc3 f5 — where Black hasn't wasted time going backward.

12. bxc3   ♝xe2
13. ♛xe2   ♞g7

13...♞f6 must be a better move, enabling Black to capture after White plays ♞e4.

14. ♞e4   f6

Black's misery deepens. He can't develop 14...♞d7 because the d-pawn hangs, or 14...♖e8 because White will leap to f6 after 15. ♝g5.

15. ♝f4   ♞e8
16. ♝h6   ...

White decided he was not winning immediately at d6, so he continued bringing up more force.

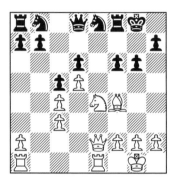

16. ...   ♞g7

White didn't lose time with 15. ♝f4 and 16. ♝h6, because Black had to play ...♞e8-g7. Black couldn't gain a move with 16...♖f7, because 17. ♞g5 wins.

17. ♖ad1   ♞a6
18. ♖d3   f5

Another hole in Black's position is created by a further pawn move, while White's pieces are fully mobile. Black knows he has to play 18...♞c7 sooner or later to involve the knight in the game, and it is rarely wrong to play a move now if you know you're bound to play it soon.

19. ♞g5   ♞c7
20. ♛e7   ...

The white queen swoops in to threaten mate, and if Black swaps, a white piece comes up with the recapture — another example of Capablanca simplifying a position to his advantage.

20. ...   ♕xe7

If 20...♘ce8, White would not take on b7, but instead play 21. ♖h3 — threatening 22. ♗xg7 — and then 21... ♕xe7 transposes to the game.

21. ♖xe7   ♘ce8
22. ♖h3   ...

Black is lost. His a8-rook was a spectator throughout.

22. ...   f4
23. ♗xg7   ♘xg7
24. ♖xh7   ♘f5
25. ♖e6   ...

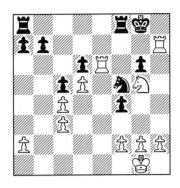

25. ...   ♖fe8

Or 25...♘g7 26. ♖xg6 ♖f7 27. ♖gh6 ♔f8 28. ♖h8+ ♔e7 29. ♖xa8.

26. ♖xg6+   1-0

Chapter 17

Mates with Minor Pieces

A bishop and knight separated by one square on the same rank or file cooperate wonderfully. The black king can't slip outside the sixth rank because the white minors cordon off a6-b6-c6, and neither can the king escape east of the d-file because the minors make a wall at c7-d7-e7-e8.

1.	♔g2	♔a7
2.	♔f3	♔b7
3.	♔f4	♔c8
4.	♔f5	♔d8
5.	♔e6	♔c8
6.	♔e7	♔b7
7.	♔d7	♔b8
8.	♗a6	♔a7
9.	♗c8	♔b8
10.	♘e7	♔a8

10...♔a7 11. ♔c7 ♔a8 12. ♗b7+ ♔a7 13. ♘c8#.

11.	♔c7	♔a7
12.	♘c6+	...

Again the minor pieces are separated by one square on the file.

12.	...	♔a8
13.	♗b7#	1-0

The "Metzger's W" checkmate pattern is beautiful. Each white piece cuts successive V's across the chessboard to corner the black king.

1.	...	♔e8
2.	♔e5	...

The king's V is f6-e5-d6.

2.	...	♔d8
3.	♔d6	♔e8
4.	♗d5	...

The bishop's V is e6-d5-c6.

4.	...	♚d8
5.	♗c6	♚c8
6.	♘f4	...

The knight's V is one square taller — because knight moves are two squares long — g6-f4-e6.

6.	...	♚d8

If the king runs the other way, then 6...♚b8 7. ♘d5 ♚a7 (7...♚c8 8. ♔e7 ♚b8 9. ♔d7 ♚a7 10. ♗b5 ♚b8 11. ♗a6 ♚a7 12. ♗c8 ♚b8 13. ♘e7 ♚a8 14. ♔c7 ♚a7 15. ♘c6+ ♚a8 16. ♗b7#) 8. ♗b5 forms the same minor-piece configuration from the first diagram. Then 8...♚b7 9. ♔d7 ♚b8 10. ♗a6 ♚a7 11. ♗c8 ♚b8 12. ♘e7 ♚a7 13. ♔c7 ♚a8 14. ♗b7+ ♚a7 15. ♘c8#.

7.	♘e6+	♚c8
8.	♔c5	...

Repeating the "W" pattern.

8.	...	♚b8
9.	♔b6	♚c8
10.	♗b5	♚b8
11.	♗a6	♚a8
12.	♘d4	♚b8
13.	♘c6+	♚a8
14.	♗b7#	1-0

This is the piece configuration from Capablanca-Corzo, 11th match game, after 36. ♘e7!:

If the other units magically vanished from the chessboard, the game might proceed:

1.	...	♚h6
2.	♔g3	♚g5
3.	♗e5	♚h5
4.	♗f6	♚h6
5.	♔g4	♚h7
6.	♔f5	♚h6
7.	♘g6!	...

Entering Metzger's W.

7.	...	♚h5

7...♚h7 8. ♘e5 ♚h6 9. ♔g4 ♚h7 10. ♔h5 ♚g8 11. ♗e7 ♚g7 12. ♔g5 ♚h7 13. ♗f8 ♚g8 14. ♔h6 ♚h7 15. ♘g4 ♚g8 16. ♔g6 ♚h8 17. ♗g7+ ♚g8 18. ♘h6#.

8.	♘f4+	♚h6
9.	♔e6	♚h7
10.	♔f7	♚h6
11.	♗e7	♚h7
12.	♗f8	♚h8
13.	♘d5	♚h7
14.	♘f6+	♚h8
15.	♗g7#	1-0

Game 54

La Habana 1901, Match (11)
White: J.R. Capablanca
Black: Juan Corzo
Queen's Pawn Game

1.	d4	...

Because this game foretold of greatness — an extraordinary effort by a 13-year-old chessplayer — it is included in every anthology of Capablanca games. Annotators wrote rapturously about the opening and early middlegame.

It's a long game, so perhaps they felt obligated to fill the dead air, but the first 25 moves or so of this game never struck me as special. In my first attempts at annotating this game, I tried hard to sound enthusiastic about the early phases, but I promised myself years ago that if I ever wrote about this game again that I would say nothing until move 25. At the moment I am compromising.

1.	...	d5
2.	♘f3	c5
3.	e3	♘c6
4.	b3	...

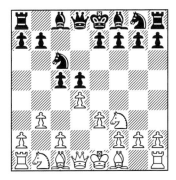

Golombek went on about the "elementary logic of youth," given that the bishop was blocked at e3, so it developed on b2. Capablanca played this Colle setup his whole life — maybe Golombek was reaching for something to say.

4.	...	e6
5.	♗b2	♘f6
6.	♘bd2	cxd4
7.	exd4	...

White must always be thinking about how to spring his bishop from behind this immobile pawn.

| 7. | ... | ♗d6 |
| 8. | ♗d3 | 0-0 |

| 9. | 0-0 | ♘h5 |

Black fails to harass the bishop by ...♘f4, but he shouldn't miss his chances to play ...♗b4.

10.	g3	f5
11.	♘e5	♘f6
12.	f4	♗xe5
13.	fxe5	♘g4
14.	♕e2	♕b6
15.	♘f3	♗d7

Black blew opportunities to play ...♘c6-b4, but ...♗c8-d7 can fit into a plan of ...a7-a6 plus ...♗d7-b5 to exchange bad bishop for good.

16.	a3	♔h8
17.	h3	♘h6
18.	♕f2	...

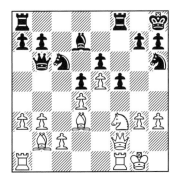

One of the terms that readers of *My System* gush over is "overprotection," which is just a fancy term for giving one's pieces mobility. While there were two pieces guarding d4, neither could move without leaving the d4-pawn to hang. 18. ♕f2 "overprotects" the pawn, after which any of the three defenders is free to move from its protection of d4.

| 18. | ... | ♘f7 |
| 19. | ♔g2 | ... |

If White's queen had moved off the g1-a7 diagonal — 19. ♕d2? for instance — White self-pins the d4-pawn, enabling Black to capture on e5. 19. ♔g2 avoids the self-pin in advance, and frees the first rank for the rooks.

| 19. ... | g5 |
| 20. g4 | ... |

If Black tries ...f5-f4, White attacks along the h-file after h3-h4.

| 20. ... | ♘e7 |
| 21. ♕e3 | ... |

A good move for a number of reasons: 1) it threatens g5, perhaps provoking ...f5-f4; 2) it removes the queen from the f-file, on which the black rook stares at her; 3) in case of ...♘g6-f4xd3, White is ready to retake with a piece move.

| 21. ... | ♖g8 |
| 22. ♖ae1 | ... |

Golombek said this move was worthy of a mature master, and perhaps it is. One of the things that happens to chess authors is that they forget what average or inexperienced players don't know. For one, 21. ♕e3 self-pinned d4, so 22. ♖ae1 broke the pin by guarding e3. Second, and more important, White can see that after an eventual ...exf5, the e5-pawn becomes a passed pawn, behind which a rook belongs.

22. ...	♘g6
23. gxf5	♘f4+
24. ♔h2	♘xd3

Black achieves ...♘xd3, but spent more time than on ...♘c6-b4xd3, while ...♗b5xd3 was preferable in order to swap the bad bishop.

| 25. ♕xd3 | exf5 |

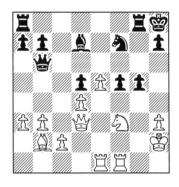

I promised myself I wouldn't include any notes to this game until this point, but every time you annotate a game, you find something more to say than you said the last time. Hopefully, it shows that you've learned something.

White is in search of a short plan, based on some feature in the position.

The player will consider:

Threats. Black has none, but ...g5-g4 and ...♗d7-b5 are moves to look out for. White has some objects of attack: e6 would fork, d5 is unguarded.

Material. Material is equal.

Pawn structure. The isolated d5-pawn is the only significant pawn weakness on the board.

Piece mobility. White is fully developed, but his bishop is blocked. Black lags in development, while his bishop is basically bad (hindered by center pawns on the same color square).

King safety. White's king is slightly more exposed, but there's little Black can do about that, given White's better center control and development (according to Kasparov's notion of judging attacking prospects by looking at the board divided between the d- and e-files, White has superior numbers). White's bishop can see the black king on the other side of the central pawn wall.

In sum, White has better center control with two center pawns against one, plus centralized major pieces. He has a lead in development, and king safety would also swing in White's favor after the center pawns cleared the diagonal — that's the feature in this position which suggests a plan. From a superior position, one should attack the enemy king by opening files — or, less often, diagonals.

26. c4   ...

Above all, 26. c4 is a threatening move.

26. ...   ♕e6

The best defense is a counterattack. 26...g4 27. ♘d2 g3+ 28. ♔g2 f4 threatens the powerful 29...♗xh3+ 30. ♔xh3 ♕h6+ 31. ♔g2 ♕h2+ 32. ♔f3 ♘g5+. In *My Chess Career*, Capablanca said 26...♕h6 is the right move, which would coordinate against h3, while eyeing the white knight if it withdraws to d2.

27. cxd5   ...

Breaking down the blocking pawn with gain of time. The game is very pretty here.

27. ...   ♕xd5
28. e6   ♗b5

If 28...♗xe6, then 29. ♖xe6!, but Black saw the win of rook for bishop by this skewer.

29. ♕xb5!   ...

The queen sacrifice enables White to clear the a1-h8 diagonal.

29. ...   ♕xb5
30. d5+   ♖g7
31. exf7

One of the difficulties in writing about classic old games is finding new words to say, or even choosing which old words to reuse. In positions where tactics prevail, chess analysis software has made annotators lazy, often falling back on what the software declares "best" instead of searching their hearts for what is "real" in a position.

31. ...   h6

Capablanca's note described Black using inactive force: 31...♖f8 coordinates Black's major pieces against f7 with 32. ♘d4 ♕xd5 33. ♖e8 ♕xf7, but White is winning on 34. ♖xf8+ ♕xf8 35. ♘xf5.

32. ♘d4   ...

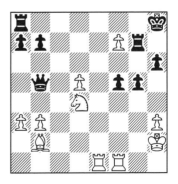

32. ...   ♕xf1

Pulling the e1-rook off the file before White plays ♖e8+ plus f8♕. The alternative is to keep the queen trained on e8 by 32...♕d7, but then 33. ♘xf5 ♕xf7 34. ♗xg7+ will win.

33. ♖xf1   ♖xf7
34. ♖xf5   ♖xf5

It would be hard to blame Black if he were rattled now, but 34...♖xf5 is a slip because the swap brings white pieces forward with threats. 34...♔g7 is an improvement.

35. ♘xf5+   ♔h7

It would have made for a less instructive game if Black had sent his king over to block the passed pawn with 35...♔g8. White is winning after 36. ♘xh6+ ♔f8 37. d6.

36. ♘e7!   ...

36. ♘e7 is as striking in its positional logic as the queen sacrifice was at move 29. The white minors cooperate to seal the black king off from helping to stop the d-pawn.

36. ♘e7 isn't a move one would find unless one both recognized the knight-and-bishop coordination and understood the importance of limiting the opponent's king's activity in the endgame.

36. ...   ♖f8
37. ♔g2   ...

Otherwise Black would activate his rook by 37...♖f2 or 37...♖f1.

37. ...   h5

Seeking to achieve some counterplay by creating a passed pawn, and at least Black's king may move now.

38. d6   g4
39. hxg4   hxg4
40. ♗e5   ♔h6
41. d7   ...

It's not a coincidence that 42. ♗c7, the next move to escort the passed pawn, remakes the powerful formation of bishop and knight separated by one square.

41. ...   ♖d8
42. ♘g8+   ♖xg8
43. ♗f6   ♔g6
44. d8♕   ♖xd8

45. ♗xd8   ...

Entering the final phase of the ending, in which two details must be kept in mind. The "rook pawn plus wrong color bishop" detail must be understood, and the more basic "to win without pawns, one must be a rook or two minor pieces ahead." In other words, if Black succeeds in exchanging both white pawns — or in removing the white b-pawn — he can draw despite being a bishop behind.

45. ...   b5

Given the constraints under which White must manage his queenside pawns, 45...b5 is a pretty good move. White is inhibited from 46. a4, because after 46...bxa4, White must not recapture, which would result in the rook-pawn-plus-wrong-bishop ending. White is also dissuaded from 46. b4, which would make the pawn on a3 vulnerable to the black king's approach.

46. ♔f2   ...

The right plan. The king goes to attack on the queenside, while the long-ranged bishop can block the g-pawn and still influence the queenside.

46. ...	**♔f5**
47. ♔e3	**♔e5**
48. ♔d3	**♔d5**
49. ♔c3	**g3**
50. ♗h4	**g2**
51. ♗f2	**a5**
52. b4	**♔e4**

The trick is 53. bxa5 ♔d5, and Black draws. The b5-pawn and black king are keeping the white king from circling around to attack the black pawns, so White marks time with

his bishop until Black has to give ground.

53. ♗b6   ...

53. ...	**♔d5**

Psychologically, 53...♔e5 is craftier because the king moved further away from the a-file, but 54. bxa5?? makes the same result geometrically: 53...♔d6 55. a6 ♔c6 with a draw.

54. ♔d3	**♔c6**
55. ♗g1	**♔d5**
56. ♗h2	**♔c6**
57. ♔d4	**a4**
58. ♔e5	**♔b6**

One of the things that makes this game great is that there were pitfalls for White along every step of the way. White had to be wary of 59. ♔d6 ♔a6 60. ♔c6 g1♕ 61. ♗xg1, drawing by stalemate.

59. ♔d5	**♔a6**
60. ♔c5	**1-0**

Chapter 18

The Arabian Mate

According to *The Art of the Checkmate*, before the rules changed in the 15th century the only pieces that moved as they do now were rook, knight, and king, so the first recorded checkmate was the Arabian Mate.

1. ♘f6   h2
2. ♖h7#   1-0

Game 55

Buenos Aires 1914
White: J.R. Capablanca
Black: Benito Villegas
Queen's Gambit Declined

1. d4   ...

This game is to Capablanca as the Paris opera house game was to Morphy. The opponent's errors are ex-ploited simply and the game is positionally logical from start to finish, while the tactics that arise are striking. But this game isn't included in some Capablanca anthologies because it was an informal game, an irrational reason to exclude a game from a collection of best games.

1. ...   d5
2. ♘f3   ...

The advance c2-c4 is the best idea for establishing a better center for White, but he doesn't have to play it now. 2. ♘f3 improves White's center control with a developing move, while avoiding Albin's 2. c4 e5, for whatever that is worth.

2. ...   ♘f6
3. e3   ...

White hasn't ruled out a bishop development to f4 or g5. Colle's scheme is to finish developing the kingside quickly, build up the power behind the e-pawn with ♘bd2, ♗f1-d3, ♖f1-e1, then unleash the power of the pieces with e3-e4. While that's going on, the game could unfold in a way to suggest the best development for the queen's bishop — sometimes it placed most effectively on b2.

3. ...   c6

4. ♗d3   ♗g4

Black's queen's bishop development might be premature. His queenside is weakened some, while the pin is ineffective.

5. c4   ...

Black's bishop development suggested that White might develop his queen to b3 to make a threat, or to c2 to break the pin. White could've settled for 5. c3, but the bishop on g4 further indicates that in the event of ... dxc4, White would like to play ♘xc4 followed by ♘ce5 to hit that bishop.

5. ...	**e6**
6. ♘bd2	**♘bd7**
7. 0-0	**♗e7**
8. ♕c2	**...**

His pin broken, Black got the notion to maneuver his bishop around to swap his "bad bishop" — hindered by center pawns on the same color squares — for White's "good bishop," but this takes too much time, and in the meantime White improves his development and center control.

8. ...	**♗h5**
9. b3	**♗g6**
10. ♗b2	**♗xd3**
11. ♕xd3	**0-0**
12. ♖ae1	**...**

White has to open the position to take advantage of his superior development. Specifically, a file should be opened for his rooks — 12. cxd5 would accomplish that aim, but 12. ♖ae1 plus 13. e4 broadens White's center as well.

12. ...	**♕c7**
13. e4	**dxe4**
14. ♘xe4	**♘xe4**
15. ♖xe4	**♗f6**

As long as White sees the threatened fork 16...♘c5, then Black is wrong not to improve the knight before the bishop with 15...♘f6.

16. ♕e3   ...

Part of the chessplayer's art is giving the opponent all the rope he needs with which to hang himself. White saw with 15...♗f6 that Black is trying to make use of the pin on the d4-pawn, but 16. ♕e3 did not break the pin, and Black is encouraged to continue.

16. ...	**c5**
17. ♘e5	**...**

17. ...   cxd4

Black was probably pleased here, seeing 18. ♗xd4 ♘xe5 19. ♗xe5 ♗xe5 20. ♖xe5 ♖fd8, where he is about equal in the endgame, even after his poor opening.

18. ♘xd7! ...

A shock, maybe.

18. ... **♛xd7**

If Black accepts the queen sacrifice with 18...dxe3, then 19. ♘xf6+ ♚h8 (19...gxf6 20. ♖g4+ ♚h8 21. ♗xf6# is Morphy's Mate) 20. ♖h4 threatens the Arabian Mate 21. ♖xh7#. Then in case of 20...h6 21. ♖xh6+ the bishop's diagonal is opened, so that 21...gxh6 22. ♘d5+ wins the queen with a winning material advantage for White.

19. ♗xd4 ...

Another point to 16. ♛e3 is that this recapture makes a threat: 20. ♗xf6 gxf6 21. ♖g4+ plus 22. ♛h6 and mate to follow.

19. ... **♗xd4**

White's recapture improves yet another piece, but Black can't support the bishop by 19...♛e7 because of 20. ♗c5, while 19...♛d8 looks very bad. Black should've played 19...♗e7, even though White's pieces hover ominously over the kingside.

20. ♖xd4 **♛c7**
21. ♖fd1 ...

White's mobilization is complete, and he has strong control of the only open file. Another trump in White's position is that his pawn majority is safe to advance — if Black pushed his pawn majority to try to make a passed pawn of his own, it would expose his king, while the white king is on the preferred side of the board for blocking the black pawns. The rest of the game is notable for White's single-mindedness in pushing the c-pawn, his potential passed pawn.

21. ... **♖fd8**

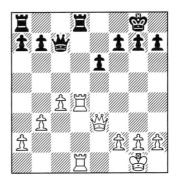

22. b4 ...

White could not steal a pawn with 22. ♖xd8+ ♖xd8 23. ♖xd8+ ♛xd8 24. ♛xa7 because of 24...♛d1#, but it's better to think that even if ...♛d1 were not checkmate that White would not bother grabbing that pawn — because that would not aid in pushing the passed pawn.

22. ... **♖xd4**
23. ♛xd4 **b6**

Trying to halt the c-pawn, while freeing the rook from its defense of a7.

24. g3 ...

Ensuring there won't be an accident on the back rank.

24. ... **♖c8**
25. ♖c1 ...

Most players could not be persuaded to relinquish control of the d-file, but making a new queen is more important, for which purpose rooks belong behind passed pawns.

25. ... **♖d8**
26. ♛e3 ...

Preventing Black from getting an aggressive rook with ...♖d2 while at the same time supporting the pawn's advance to c5.

26. ... **♚f8**

27. c5	bxc5
28. ♕e4	...

The first pretty move in the major-piece ending. An immediate 28. bxc5 ♕c6 would block the pawn from its next step.

28. ...	♖d5
29. bxc5	...

Not 29. ♖xc5 because it doesn't create a passed pawn.

29. ...	g6

29...♖xc5 loses to 30. ♕b4. 29...g6 preserves the h-pawn, but White would not have taken it even if he could.

30. c6	♔g7
31. a4!	...

The second lovely move in the ending. White's plan to break down the blockade is ♕e4-b4-b7, but if he plays it too soon, then ...♕xb7 cxb7 ♖b5 puts the black rook behind the passed pawn. 31. a4 cuts off the rook.

31. ...	♖d6
32. ♕e5+	♔f8

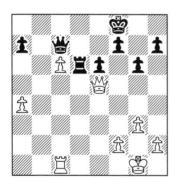

33. ♕xd6+! 1-0

White's second queen sacrifice is merely the fastest way to promoting the c-pawn.

Game 56

Hastings 1934
White: George Norman
Black: J.R. Capablanca
King's Indian Defense

1. d4	♘f6
2. c4	g6

This was the only King's Indian Defense Capablanca played in a tournament. It's been suggested that Capablanca wanted to take a break from the Nimzo-Indian following his previous game with Black, in which Lilienthal successfully sacrificed his queen: 1. d4 ♘f6 2. c4 e6 3. ♘c3 ♗b4 4. a3 ♗xc3+ 5. bxc3 b6 6. f3 d5 7. ♗g5 h6 8. ♗h4 ♗a6 9. e4 ♗xc4 10. ♗xc4 dxc4 11. ♕a4+ ♕d7 12. ♕xc4 ♕c6 13. ♕d3 ♘bd7 14. ♘e2 ♖d8 15. 0-0 a5 16. ♕c2 ♕c4 17. f4 ♖c8 18. f5 e5 19. dxe5 ♕xe4 20. exf6! ♕xc2 21. fxg7 ♖g8 22. ♘d4, when White threatens the queen and also a checkmate akin to the *épaulettes* mate.

3. ♘c3	♗g7
4. e4	d6
5. f3	...

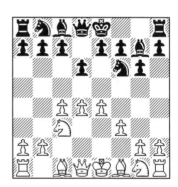

Sämisch's move strengthens the white pawn center, shields a bishop on e3 from ...♘g4, and restricts the black queen bishop.

5. ...   ♘bd7

The queen sacrifice 5...0-0 6. ♗e3 e5 7. d5 ♘h5 8. ♕d2 ♕h4+ 9. g3 ♘xg3 10. ♕f2 ♘xf1 11. ♕xh4 ♘xe3 12. ♗e2 ♘xc4 is another of Bronstein's inventions.

6. ♗e3   e5
7. d5   a5

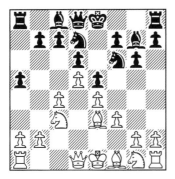

One of the notes we see often — but I didn't understand for a long time — is "Securing the outpost," which means that after Black plays ...♘d7-c5, White can't easily play b2-b4 to kick the knight.

On that subject, and related to one of this book's main themes, one of Capablanca's rare mistakes arose when he played White against Bogoljubow's King's Indian at Karlsbad 1929. After 1. d4 ♘f6 2. c4 g6 3. g3 ♗g7 4. ♗g2 0-0 5. e4 d6 6. ♘e2 ♘bd7 7. 0-0 e5 8. d5, Bogoljubow should have played 8...a5 to secure his c5 outpost, but he thought a threat against the e4-pawn would afford him time to play ...a5 on his next turn, so he played 8...♘c5.

However, 9...♘cxe4 was a threat Capablanca could have ignored — because 10. f3 wins a piece — but he erred with 9. ♘bc3 instead of 9. b4.

8. ♗d3   ♘c5
9. ♗c2   ...

It wouldn't be bad to ignore the threat to swap the bishop and play 9. ♘ge2, perhaps. The d3-bishop is hindered by center pawns while the c5-knight is Black's best minor. Also, a trade on d3 develops the white queen for free. The arguments against the trade are that Black's position is relatively cramped, so Black would be relieved by an exchange, and that Black's eventual freeing move is ...f7-f5, so White would like to have his bishop watching over the square.

9. ...   ♘h5
10. ♕d2   f5
11. ♗xc5   ...

An odd decision, trading bishop for knight in a worse circumstance — good bishop for knight, and not gaining time with a recapture — than ... ♘xd3 would have been a few moves before. More typical would have been b2-b3, a2-a3, b3-b4 to chase the knight, and eventually c4-c5 to break the queenside open.

11. ...   dxc5

Another flaw in White's judgment is that c5 is occupied by a black pawn, so if White is going to operate on the queenside, he has to break through b4, a square now controlled by two black pawns.

12. ♕f2   b6
13. ♘ge2   0-0
14. b3   ♘f6
15. ♕e3   ♘e8
16. 0-0   ♘d6

The knight is well placed on d6, hitting the white pawn chain in two places, and supporting black pawns on f5 (and perhaps b5).

17. a4 ...

White is misguided. By locking up the queenside, the fight shifts over to the kingside where Black has more maneuvering room.

17. ... &d7
18. &ad1 ♛h4

Among the three safe queen moves off the first rank, only ...♛h4 is threatening in nature — Black might continue with ...&g7-h6.

19. ♛f2 ♛g5
20. ♛e1 ...

The move ...fxe4 was not yet a threat, but White thought it prudent to move his queen off the f-file, while an alternative move that improves White's position is not obvious.

20. ... &ae8

21. &h1 &h8

Whereas 21. &h1 seemed to mark time for White, Black's 21...&h8 is more reasoned. In case of a pawn exchange on f5, the g-file comes open for Black, and g8 is now open for a rook. Or if Black expands on the kingside with a g-pawn advance, he will want a rook on g8 in that event also.

22. ♘g3 &h6

23. ♘b5 ...

White grows bored waiting for the game to come to him, so he lashes out mistakenly. The result is a crack in his queenside pawn structure and a point of attack for Black.

23. ... &xb5
24. axb5 ♛h4

Black is envisioning ...&h6-f4 plus ...&xg3 and ...a5-a4, after which White will have weak pawns all over the board.

25. ♘e2 ♛xe1
26. &dxe1 a4

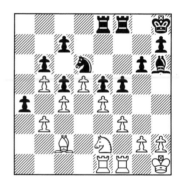

27. ♘g3 ...

A silly move. When White played 25. ♘e2, wasn't it in order to avoid ...&h6-f4xg3? Better would've been 27. exf5 gxf5 28. &a1.

27. ... &f4
28. ♘e2 ...

Losing a pawn. Again, White needs to rush to the a-file with 28. exf5 gxf5 29. &a1. In any endgame with rooks, the rooks must be active at all costs.

28. ... axb3
29. ♘xf4 exf4
30. &xb3 fxe4
31. fxe4 ♘xe4

White's game is a mess. He's a pawn down, while his bishop is the worst kind of bishop, passively placed behind pawns on squares of its same color. He can't even play 32. ♖a1 because 32...♘d2 wins material.

32. ♗a2   ♘d2
33. ♖xe8   ♖xe8
34. ♖d1   ♖e2

35. ♗b1   f3
0-1

Black has crushing threats. For starters, Black has 36...fxg2+ 37. ♔g1 ♘f3#. In case of 36. g4, then Black queens following 36...f2 and 37...♖e1+. Finally, 36. gxf3 ♘xf3 followed by 37...♖xh2# is the Arabian Mate.

Chapter 19

One More Thing

At Apple shareholder meetings and Macworld Expos over the years, when Apple boss Steve Jobs was about to unveil a blockbuster surprise at the end of his keynote address, he would say offhandedly, "One more thing...."

At the chessboard, "one more thing" is the last piece thrown into the attack, that final chunk of firewood that burns the opponent down. In some of the prettiest games, the last available bit of new force is a king move by the attacking side.

Game 57

New Orleans 1858
Blindfold simultaneous exhibition
White: Paul Morphy
Black: A.N. Other
Evans Gambit

1.	e4	e5
2.	♘f3	♘c6
3.	♗c4	♗c5
4.	b4	...

The Evans Gambit has a positional sensibility that belies its Romantic heritage. For the price of a mere b-pawn, White gains center control and room for his queenside pieces.

Kasparov was moved to play the Evans Gambit at the highest level.

4.	...	♗xb4
5.	c3	♗a5
6.	d4	exd4
7.	0-0	...

7.	...	dxc3

Enabling White to develop ♕d1-b3 with a double threat. Much better is 7. ... ♘ge7 8. cxd4 d5, fighting for control of the center while ...♗a5 has prevented 9. ♘c3 or 9. ♖e1.

8.	♗a3	...

8. ♕b3 is preferable because leaving the bishop on c1 inhibits Black from guarding f7 with ...♘h6.

8.	...	d6

9.	♕b3	♘h6
10.	♘xc3	♗xc3

Otherwise the knight might hop away to leave the bishop staring into space, but this is the fourth move for the bishop.

11.	♕xc3	0-0
12.	♖ad1	...

The d6-pawn is pinned both on the file and on the diagonal. 13. e5 would be a punishing continuation.

12.	...	♘g4
13.	h3	...

A remarkable little move, prompting Black to play the move he wanted to play, but White also desires ...♘ge5, so that he can swap his own knight before introducing unused force on the f-file.

13.	...	♘ge5
14.	♘xe5	♘xe5
15.	♗e2	...

Better than 15. ♗b3, which can be opposed by ...♗e6.

15.	...	f5

A poor move, exposing the king and opening the position while he trails in development. In *Masters of the Chessboard*, Réti suggested 15... f6, restraining White's e4-e5 advance.

16.	f4	♘c6
17.	♗c4+	♔h8
18.	♗b2	♕e7
19.	♖de1	...

More far-seeing than 19. ♖fe1, because if White plays exf5, a rook on d1 bites rock at d6.

19.	...	♖f6
20.	exf5	♕f8

21.	♖e8!	♕xe8
22.	♕xf6	♕e7
23.	♕xg7+	♕xg7
24.	f6!	...

In truth, Black played 24...♕xg2+ 25. ♔xg2 ♗xh3+ 26. ♔xh3 h5 27. ♖g1 1-0, which completely ruined the aesthetics.

Reti suggested this finish in his notes:

24.	...	♕f8
25.	f7+	♘e5
26.	fxe5	h5
27.	e6+	♔h7
28.	♗d3+	♔h6
29.	♖f6+	♔g5
30.	♖g6+	♔f4

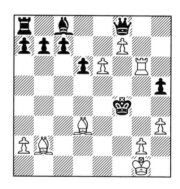

31. ♔f2!

Introducing one more thing with the threat 32. g3#.

31	...	h4
32.	♖g4#	1-0

When sharing this game, show it as if Réti's line actually took place — in other words, don't let the facts get in the way of a good story (or let the moves get in the way of a good chess game).

Game 58

New York 1909, Match (23)
White: Frank Marshall
Black: J.R. Capablanca
Queen's Gambit Declined

1.	d4	...

It was Marshall-Capablanca, 23rd match game, that woke me up to Purdy's instruction that to play this game passably well, we must recognize the unreality of the opponent's unreal threats.

Until a chessplayer learns to stand his ground while the Black Hat fires at the dusty street, he is doomed to be the Comic Relief character who dances up and down. When the chessplayer starts to ignore unreal threats, he can then be Gary Cooper Riding into the Sunset with Grace Kelly.

1.	...	d5
2.	c4	...

For 600 years, 2. c4 has been a strong bid for advantage, broadening White's stance in the center, and perhaps deflecting or capturing Black's center pawn. For just as long, Black has pondered symmetrical openings as a try for equality, but 2...c5 here has not gained much trust.

2.	...	e6
3.	♘c3	c5

Tarrasch got some ridicule for saying that his defense to the Queen's Gambit was the only correct one, but he wasn't too far wrong. Having interpolated 2...e6, Black can maintain his center pawn in case White plays 4. cxd5, while 3...c5 makes the same challenge to the center that White made at move 2.

In other words, the Tarrasch Defense is an improved attempt at a symmetrical defense to the Queen's Gambit. Spassky and Kasparov both played the Tarrasch in world championship matches.

4.	cxd5	exd5

4...cxd4 5. ♕xd4 ♘c6 is a gambit worth exploring.

5.	♘f3	♘c6
6.	g3	...

The idea that cast a shadow over the Tarrasch Defense is that the bishop on g2 presses on the unsupported pawn at d5.

6.	...	♗e6

The bishop is passively placed here. Capablanca said he was intrigued with Mieses's idea at move 9, but this was his last experiment with the Tarrasch.

7.	♗g2	♗e7
8.	0-0	♘f6
9.	♗g5	♘e4

The idea is the same in Lasker's defense to the Queen's Gambit (1. d4 d5 2. c4 e6 3. ♘c3 ♘f6 4. ♗g5 ♗e7 5. ♘f3 0-0 6. e3 h6 7. ♗h4 ♘e4) to ease Black's game by effecting a couple of exchanges; but does that idea make as much sense in Tarrasch's defense?

Black played 3...c5 to give himself more space, so he is freer than in the orthodox lines. Further, the price Black pays in the Tarrasch is taking on the isolated d-pawn, and in general, when playing with an isolated pawn, one wants to avoid exchanges, which intensify the pawn's isolation.

10. ♗xe7   ♕xe7
11. ♘e5   ...

White based his play on a mistaken evaluation at move 15, else he might have tried 11. ♖c1, using an inactive rook that can recapture on c3 or discover an attack on c5. Not 11. ♘xe4 dxe4, which solves the problem of Black's weak d-pawn.

11. ...   ♘xd4
12. ♘xe4   dxe4
13. e3   ♘f3+
14. ♘xf3   exf3
15. ♕xf3   ...

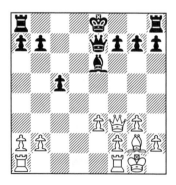

This is the position White foresaw when he played 11. ♘e5. He has a slight lead in development, and he is

counting on the threat to b7 to further delay Black's mobilization.

15. ...   0-0!

Evening the development, because White's threat is unreal. 16. ♕xb7 ♕xb7 17. ♗xb7 ♖ab8 plus 18...♖xb2 is good for Black.

16. ♖fc1   ...

Given the state of the match, and the sudden realization that he misjudged this position, the American champion played the rest in frustration. 16. ♖fd1 was a more reasoned move.

16. ...   ♖ab8
17. ♕e4   ...

If White continued with 17. ♗h3, it could result in a capture or two on e6, and then an isolated pawn for Black. Black sidestepped that, probably as much to avoid material simplification as to avoid the pawn weakness.

17. ...   ♕c7
18. ♖c3   ...

As we've noted before, the basis for the "rooks belong behind passed pawns" principle is that when the passed pawn (in this case, the black c-pawn is a passed pawn in the making) advances, a rook behind it gains scope, while a rook in front of it loses scope. White played 18. ♖c3, disconnecting his rooks, when he had to know that ...c4 was coming soon to shorten the rook's view. An uncharacteristic move for Marshall, whose pieces usually soared.

18. ...   b5
19. a3   ...

Though Black just pushed the b-pawn, White wasn't thinking about its further advance. 19. a3 frees the a1-rook from its defense of a2.

19. ...   c4

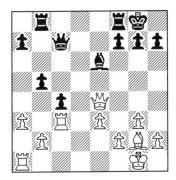

20. ♗f3   ...

20. ♖d1 ♖fd8 21. ♖cc3 adheres to the same plan, but it would have admitted that 18. ♖c3 was silly, and chessplayers have a hard time with that. When chessplayers discover they have made a bad move, sometimes they design following moves solely to lend credence to the bad move.

20. ...   ♖fd8
21. ♖d1   ♖xd1+
22. ♗xd1   ♖d8
23. ♗f3   ...

So Black was enabled to play ...♖d8 as a threatening move, while the white rook is still poorly placed on c3.

23. ...   g6
24. ♕c6   ♕e5

Chessplayers could save a fortune in thinking time by avoiding exchanges that improve enemy pieces. 24...♕xc6 25. ♗xc6 brings the bishop to a threatening position.

25. ♕e4   ♕xe4

Whereas this queen swap does not improve the bishop.

26. ♗xe4   ♖d1+
27. ♔g2   a5

Using inactive force. The black pawn majority goes forward with the plan of ...b5-b4 to kick the blockading rook, and then ...c4-c3 to push the passed pawn.

28. ♖c2   b4
29. axb4   axb4
30. ♗f3   ♖b1

The first job for any rook in an endgame with rooks is to attack things. The second job is to take things, because that frees the rook to attack other things. The third job is to limit enemy mobility. 30...♖b1 curbs the white rook's mobility to the second rank, so that after ...b4-b3, the rook could not abandon the b2-pawn.

31. ♗e2   b3
32. ♖d2   ♖c1

The rook's first job is to threaten things. 32...♖c1 prepares ...♖c2, which threatens things.

33. ♗d1   c3
34. bxc3   b2
35. ♖xb2   ♖xd1
36. ♖c2   ...

36. ...   ♗f5

The rook's first job is to threaten.

36...♗f5 chases the white rook from the c-file, so that the black rook can threaten.

| 37. ♖b2 | ♖c1 |
| 38. ♖b3 | ♗e4+ |

A neat move. 39. f3 loses a pawn to 39...♖c2+, while White's alternative enables Black to weave a mating net.

| 39. ♔h3 | ♖c2 |
| 40. f4 | h5 |

Threatening to close the net with 41...♗f5+ 42. ♔h4 ♖xh2+ 43. ♔g5 ♔g7! (one more thing, as in Morphy's blindfold simul gem) with mating ideas like 44...f6# or 44...h4 45. gxh4 ♖xh4 plus 46...♖h5#.

41. g4	hxg4+
42. ♔xg4	♖xh2
43. ♖b4	f5+

Using inactive force. The pawn on f5 performs the function that the h5-pawn used to do: patching the g4-hole in the mating net.

44. ♔g3	♖e2
45. ♖c4	♖xe3+
46. ♔h4	...

Enabling a shorter and shinier finish than moving the king to the second rank, when Black would play ...♖f3, ...♖xf4, and promote a pawn.

| 46. ... | ♔g7 |
| 47. ♖c7+ | ♔f6 |

Most precise. 47...♔h6 allows White another spite check by ♖c8 plus ♖h8+.

48. ♖d7	♗g2
49. ♖d6+	♔g7
0-1	

Bibliography

Bronstein, David. *Zurich International Chess Tournament 1953*, Dover Publications, 1979

Capablanca, José Raúl. *Chess Fundamentals*, Harcourt Brace, 1921

Capablanca, José Raúl. *My Chess Career*, Bell and Sons, 1920

Euwe, Max, and Meiden, Walter. *Chess Master vs. Chess Amateur*, David McKay, 1953

Fischer, Bobby, Margulies, Dr. Stuart, and Mosenfelder, Donn. *Bobby Fischer Teaches Chess*, Xerox, 1966

Golombek, Harry. *Capablanca's Hundred Best Games*, International Chess Enterprises, 1997

Khalifman, Alexander. *Capablanca I: 1907-1926*, Chess Stars, 1997

Khalifman, Alexander. *Capablanca II: 1927-1942*, Chess Stars, 1997

Purdy, C.J.S. *Fine Art of Chess Annotation and Other Thoughts*, Vol. 1, Thinkers' Press, 1992

Renaud, Georges, and Kahn, Victor. *The Art of the Checkmate*, Simon and Schuster, 1953

Réti, Richard. *Masters of the Chessboard*, Whittlesey House, 1932

Winter, Edward. *Capablanca: A Compendium of Games, Notes, Articles, Correspondence, Illustrations and Other Rare Archival Materials on the Cuban Chess Genius José Raúl Capablanca*, MacFarland, 1989

Index of Players

Numbers refer to games

Openings Index

About the Author

Frisco Del Rosario is the only chess teacher to win the *San Jose Mercury News* award as Teacher of the Week. In 2005, he was named national chess journalist of the year for authoring *A First Book of Morphy* and launching the *Success Chess School Dragon*. He is the San Francisco Chess Examiner at examiner.com, and 2009 champion of the Kolty Chess Club in Silicon Valley, where he lectures weekly. He also writes about basketball.